Freshwater Fishes of Texas

by
Earl W. Chilton II, Ph.D.

Illustrations by
Nancy McGowan
Clemente Guzman
Jared Faulk
Diana Peebles
Rob Fleming

TEXAS PARKS AND WILDLIFE PRESS

Publisher and Editor: Georg Zappler
Art Director: Pris Martin
Design: Debra Morgan
Printing Coordination: Mike Diver

**TEXAS
PARKS &
WILDLIFE**

Inland Fisheries Division
©1997 Texas Parks and Wildlife Press

ISBN: 1-885696-23-X

Contents

Introduction 1

Sunfish—Centrarchidae

Guadalupe Bass 2
Largemouth Bass 4
Spotted Bass 6
Smallmouth Bass 8
Warmouth 10
Green Sunfish 12
Redear Sunfish 14
Longear Sunfish 16
Bluegill 18
White Crappie 20
Black Crappie 22

Temperate Basses—Percichthyidae

Striped Bass 24
White Bass 26
Yellow Bass 28

Cichlids—Cichlidae

Rio Grande Cichlid 30
Blue Tilapia 32

Catfish—Ictaluridae

Flathead Catfish 34
Black Bullhead 36
Yellow Bullhead 38
Channel Catfish 40
Blue Catfish 42

Contents (Continued)

Gars—Lepisosteidae

Alligator Gar 44

Shortnose Gar 46

Spotted Gar 48

Longnose Gar 50

Suckers—Catostomidae

Smallmouth Buffalo 52

Bigmouth Buffalo 54

Drums—Sciaenidae

Freshwater Drum 56

Minnows—Cyprinidae

Common Carp 58

Grass Carp 60

Golden Shiner 62

Blacktail Shiner 64

Red Shiner 66

Texas Shiner 68

Fathead Minnow 70

Herrings—Clupeidae

Gizzard Shad 72

Threadfin Shad 74

Bowfins—Amiidae

Bowfin 76

Eels—Anguillidae

American Eel 78

Contents (Continued)

Pikes—Esocidae
    Chain Pickerel 80

Trout—Salmonidae
    Rainbow Trout 82

Paddlefishes—Polyodontidae
    Paddlefish 84

Perches—Percidae
    Greenthroat Darter 86
    Walleye 88

Silversides—Atherinidae
    Inland Silverside 90

Livebearers—Poeciliidae
    Western Mosquitofish 92

Glossary 94

References 96

Acknowledgments 98

When people think of Texas, abundant water is perhaps the last thing that comes to mind. Those who have never visited the state or those who have only been to west Texas are more likely to conjure up mental images of cowboys, cactus and dust. However, despite its dry image, an image well deserved in the western half of the state, Texas actually has more surface water than all but two other states, Minnesota and Alaska. Approximately 800 public impoundments and 80,000 miles of rivers and streams total about 1.7 million acres of water.

Texas' numerous impoundments provide an abundance of opportunities for water-related activities. Fishing, especially for black bass, catfish, crappie, striped bass and white bass, is extremely popular in many areas of the state. Black bass fishing is considered among the best in the U.S., but Texas also boasts a wide variety of other sportfish species, and water-related recreation is not limited to fishing. Swimming, boating, skiing and simply enjoying the scenery are also exceptionally popular in the state. However, no matter what the activity, if it is water related, one is likely to encounter fish. Therefore, the purpose of this booklet is to provide information about some of the more common fish species Texans and their guests are likely to encounter, as well as a number of species which are either unique to Texas or which may simply be interesting to many people. This booklet is not meant to be a comprehensive list of all Texas fish species.

Guadalupe Bass—*Micropterus treculi* [Vaillant and Bocourt]

Guadalupe Bass
Micropterus treculi (Vaillant and Bocourt)*

Other Names: Black bass, Guadalupe spotted bass

* Names in parentheses, after the scientific name, refer to the person or persons who first described the species.

Guadalupe Bass—*Micropterus treculi* (Vaillant and Bocourt)

Distribution: The Guadalupe bass is found only in Texas and has been named the official state fish. It is endemic to the northern and eastern Edwards Plateau including headwaters of the San Antonio River, the Guadalupe River above Gonzales, the Colorado River north of Austin and portions of the Brazos River drainage. Relatively small populations can also be found outside the Edwards Plateau, primarily in the lower Colorado River, and introduced populations exist in the Nueces River system. Typically, Guadalupe bass are found in flowing water, whereas largemouth bass are found in quiet water.

Description: The Guadalupe bass, like other "black bass" including largemouth, smallmouth, and spotted bass, is not a true bass at all; it is a member of the sunfish family Centrarchidae. *Micropterus*, meaning "small fin" in Greek, is a rather unfortunate misnomer arising from a defective "type" specimen in which the posterior rays of the soft dorsal fin seemed to form a small separate fin due to an injury; *treculi* refers to Trecul the French compatriot of Vaillant and Bocourt. Trecul actually caught the specimen. The Guadalupe bass is generally green in color and may be distinguished from similar species found in Texas in that it doesn't have vertical bars like smallmouth bass, its jaw doesn't extend beyond the eyes as in largemouth bass, and coloration extends much lower on the body than in spotted bass. The species has diamond-shaped markings on the sides, and the scales above the anal fin have spots which blur together to form stripes.

Biology: Both males and females become sexually mature when they are 1 year old. Guadalupe bass spawning begins as early as March and continues through May and June. A secondary spawn is possible in late summer or early fall. Like all other black bass, Guadalupe bass build gravel nests for spawning, preferably in shallow water. Similar to spotted bass and smallmouth bass, males tend to build nests in areas with higher flow rates than largemouth bass. When a male has successfully attracted a female to the nest, she may lay from 400 to over 9,000 eggs. The female is then chased away and the male stands guard over the developing eggs. After hatching, the fry feed on invertebrates and switch to piscivory as they grow older. Very young fish and older adults tend to include more invertebrates in their diet than do largemouth bass. On the other hand, juveniles and younger adults eat more fish than do largemouth bass. Hybridization with stocked smallmouth bass has become a serious problem in some areas. As a result TPWD has halted smallmouth bass stockings in areas where Guadalupe bass may be affected. Additionally, studies are underway to re-establish pure Guadalupe bass in problem areas.

Angling Importance: Guadalupe bass do not grow to large size because they are adapted to small streams. However, a propensity for fast-flowing water, and their ability to utilize fast water to their advantage when hooked, make them a desirable sportfish species. Their preference for small streams enhances their allure to anglers because of the attractive natural settings in which small streams are usually found. Specimens in excess of 3.5 pounds have been landed by anglers.

Largemouth Bass—*Micropterus salmoides* (Lacépède)

Largemouth Bass
Micropterus salmoides (Lacépède)

Other Names: Black bass, green trout, bigmouth bass, lineside bass

Largemouth Bass—*Micropterus salmoides* (Lacépède)

Distribution: Largemouth bass were originally distributed throughout most of what is now the United States east of the Rockies, with limited populations in southeastern Canada and northeastern Mexico. However, because of its importance as a game species it has now been introduced into many other areas worldwide, including nearly all of Mexico, and south into Central and South America. The species prefers clear quiet water with aquatic vegetation, but survives quite well in a variety of environments. It is usually common or abundant wherever populations have been established. Two subspecies of largemouth bass exist in Texas. The native subspecies, Northern largemouth bass *Micropterus salmoides salmoides*, is found in all natural waters except for some parts of the Panhandle, and a second subspecies, Florida largemouth bass *Micropterus salmoides floridanus*, from peninsular Florida, has been extensively stocked in state waters because of its propensity to produce more trophy-sized individuals.

Description: Florida largemouth bass are visually indistinguishable from native largemouth bass (although they may be distinguished by genetic testing procedures). Both are usually green with dark blotches that form a horizontal stripe along the middle of the fish on either side. The underside ranges in color from light green to almost white. The dorsal fin is almost divided with the anterior portion containing 9 spines, and the posterior portion containing 12-13 soft rays. Largemouth bass may be distinguished from other black basses in that the upper jaw reaches far beyond the rear margin of the eye. *Micropterus* is Greek, meaning "small fin" [see Guadalupe bass for further explanation]. *Salmoides* is from the Greek "salmo" meaning "trout" and refers to the fact that largemouth bass have been considered by some, troutlike in appearance.

Biology: In Texas spawning begins in the spring when water temperatures reach about 60°F. Because of Texas' size this can occur as early as February or as late as May, depending on location within the state. Largemouth bass prefer to nest in quiet, more vegetated water than other black bass, but will use any substrate besides soft mud, including submerged logs. Nests are usually built in two to eight feet of water. As in Guadalupe bass, once the female has laid eggs (2,000 to 43,000) in the nest, she is chased away by the male who then guards the eggs. The young, called fry, hatch in five to ten days and remain in a school. Male largemouth bass continue to guard their fry for several days after hatching. At about two inches in length, the young fish become active predators. Fry feed primarily on

zooplankton and insect larvae. Adults feed extensively on other fish and large invertebrates such as crayfish.

Angling Importance: The largemouth bass is by far the most sought-after fish in Texas. When anglers were asked to "name the fish you prefer to catch in freshwater in Texas," they chose largemouth bass three to one over striped bass, four to one over white bass, nearly five to one over channel catfish, and nearly ten to one over flathead catfish and white crappie. Because of the strong interest in largemouth bass fishing there are hundreds of clubs in Texas devoted to bass angling and conservation. A 1995 survey indicated the rate at which 10-pound bass are caught in Texas is over 13 times the rate in Florida, a state renowned for its bass fishing. Over the last sixty years only one state, California, has reported the capture of bass larger than those reported from Texas. As of 1996, the state-record fish was captured from Lake Fork in 1992 and weighed 18.18 pounds; its length was 25.5 inches.

Spotted Bass
Micropterus punctulatus (Rafinesque)

Other Names: Kentucky spotted bass, spotted black bass

Spotted Bass—*Micropterus punctulatus* (Rafinesque)

Distribution: Spotted bass are distributed throughout the Ohio River basin as well as the central and lower Mississippi River basin. The species may be found in Gulf Coast states from Texas east to Florida. In Texas spotted bass are native to portions of east Texas from the Guadalupe River to the Red River, exclusive of the Edwards Plateau region.

Description: *Micropterus* is Greek, meaning "small fin" [see Guadalupe bass for further explanation]. The species epithet *punctulatus*, Latin for "dotted," refers to rows of dark spots on the lower sides. Unlike largemouth bass, the upper lip does not extend beyond the eye. Coloration is similar to that of Guadalupe bass, but does not extend as low on the body, and the lateral stripe is not obscured by barring. Spotted bass may be confused with smallmouth bass.

Biology: Spotted bass have been considered intermediate between largemouth and small-mouth bass. They seem to be segregated from largemouth and smallmouth bass by habitat type. Spotted bass tend to be found in areas with more current than largemouth bass. However, they usually inhabit areas that are too warm, turbid, and sluggish for smallmouth bass. In general, although a large proportion reach maturity within a year, spotted bass found in spawning areas are usually three to four years old. Rock or gravel are usually chosen as suitable spawning areas at water temperatures of 57–74°F. Nest depths may vary widely. Females may lay between 1,150 and 47,000 eggs. Males guard the eggs during incubation, and for up to four weeks after they have hatched. As young fish grow their diet shifts from zooplankton to insects, and finally to fish and crayfish.

Angling Importance: Despite the fact that spotted bass are not nearly as large and numerous as largemouth bass (in Texas their maximum size is less than one-third that of largemouth bass), they are excellent fighters. Spotted bass are very popular in east Texas, particularly in the Sabine, Neches and Cypress Rivers. Known maximum size in Texas exceeds 5.5 pounds.

Slot-limit fishing regulations may be used when there is an overabundance of small fish in a body of water. For example, a 14–21 slot for bass, which allows anglers to harvest fish 14 inches or less as well as 21 inches and more, may serve a triple purpose. Overabundant small fish, which are using up resources and therefore inhibiting growth overall are harvested. Valuable reproducing 14–21 inch fish are protected from harvest. Meanwhile, harvest of trophy-sized fish over 21 inches is allowed.

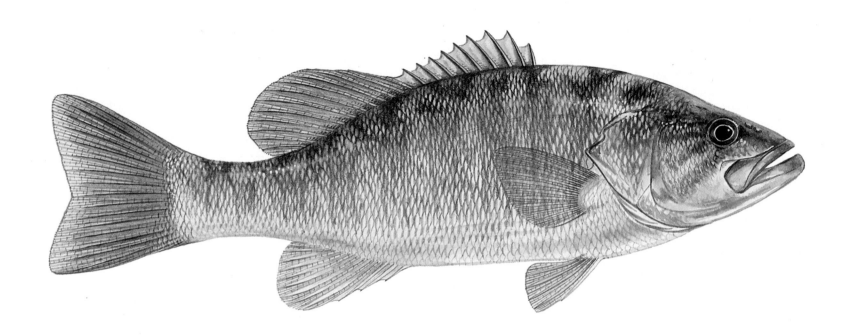

Smallmouth Bass
Micropterus dolomieu (Lacépède)

Other Names: Brown bass, brownie, bronze bass

Smallmouth Bass—*Micropterus dolomieu* (Lacépède)

Distribution: Smallmouth bass originally ranged north into Minnesota and southern Quebec, south to the Tennessee River in Alabama and west to eastern Oklahoma and southwestern Arkansas. Today there are few states, east or west of the Rocky Mountains, where populations have not become established. Florida and Louisiana are two states that appear not to have any smallmouth bass. In Texas they have been stocked in numerous areas, particularly streams of the Edwards Plateau.

Description: Smallmouth bass are generally greenish-brown to bronze-brown with dark vertical bands rather than a horizontal band or diamond shaped blotches along the sides. There are 13–15 soft rays in the dorsal fin, and the upper jaw never extends beyond the eye. *Micropterus* is Greek, meaning "small fin" [see Guadalupe bass for further explanation]. The species epithet *dolomieu* refers to the French mineralogist M. Dolomieu.

Biology: Smallmouth bass prefer large (greater than 100 acres; more that 30 feet deep) clear-water lakes and cool streams with clear water and gravel substrate. In small streams activity may be limited to just one stream pool or extend into several. Spawning occurs in the spring. When water temperatures

approach 60°F males move into spawning areas. Nests are usually located near shore in lakes, or downstream from boulders (or some other obstruction that offers protection against strong current) in streams. Mature females may contain 2,000–15,000 golden-yellow eggs. Males may spawn with several females on a single nest. On average each nest contains about 2,500 eggs, but nests may contain as many as 10,000 eggs. Eggs hatch in about 10 days if water temperatures are in the mid-50s (°F), but can hatch in 2–3 days if temperatures are in the mid-70s (°F). Males guard the nest from the time eggs are laid until fry begin to disperse, a period of up to a month. As in other black bass, fry begin to feed on zooplankton, switching to insect larvae, and finally fish and crayfish as they grow. Unfortunately, smallmouth bass hybridize easily with Guadalupe bass, and should not be stocked in areas where the genetic integrity of the state fish would be compromised.

Angling Importance: Because of their reputation in other parts of the U.S. as an excellent sportfish, smallmouth bass have been introduced into a number of Texas reservoirs and streams. Minnows, crayfish and alderfly larvae (hellgrammites) are among the most successful live baits used. Smallmouth bass now rank among the top 15 most preferred species. Known maximum size in Texas exceeds 7.5 pounds.

Warmouth
Lepomis gulosus (Cuvier)

Other Names: Goggle-eye, warmouth bass

Warmouth—*Lepomis gulosus* (Cuvier)

Distribution: The warmouth ranges from Wisconsin to south Texas, and from the east coast of the U.S. to west Texas. The species is found throughout Texas with the exception of plains streams in the Panhandle.

Description: The warmouth is very similar to rock bass and green sunfish in that it is large-mouthed and heavy-bodied. Consequently, these species are often confused with each other. Adult warmouths are dark, with mottled brown coloration, often with a purple hue. Ventral areas are generally golden, and males have a bright orange spot at the base of the dorsal fin. Warmouth have three spines in the anal fin, 10 spines in the dorsal fin, and small teeth are present on the tongue. *Lepomis*, the generic name, is Greek and means "scaled gill cover," and the species epithet *gulosus* is Latin, meaning "large-mouthed."

Biology: Warmouth may spawn from spring through the summer, with a peak in May or June. As with other sunfish, they are nest builders. However, they do not nest in large groups (or "beds") as some other species do. Males guard their nests vigorously until fry swim away. In general, warmouth prefer complex habitat with aquatic vegetation, sunken logs, stumps, etc. Young fish feed on insect larvae and switch to small fish, snails and crayfish as they grow.

Angling Importance: Warmouth are most abundant in the eastern regions of the state, hence that is where "goggle-eye" fishing is concentrated. Spring is the preferred time period for warmouth fishing, and minnows or crayfish are the preferred bait. Fish up to 1.3 pounds have been landed in Texas.

Green Sunfish
Lepomis cyanellus (Rafinesque)

Other Names: Goggle-eye, rock bass, branch perch, black perch, sunny, sun perch

Green Sunfish—*Lepomis cyanellus* (Rafinesque)

Distribution: Originally the distribution of green sunfish appears to have been limited to the central plains west of the Appalachian Mountains and east of the Rocky Mountains, including northeastern Mexico. However, due to numerous introductions, the species has become nearly ubiquitous over much of the U.S. with the exception of Florida and parts of the northwest. Green sunfish are found throughout Texas.

Description: The green sunfish, like warmouth, has a large mouth and a heavy, black bass body shape. Consequently, it is often confused with warmouth and rock bass. The body is dark green, almost blue, dorsally, fading to lighter green on the sides, and yellow to white ventrally. Faint vertical bars are apparent on the sides. Some scales have turquoise spots. *Lepomis*, the generic name, is Greek and means "scaled gill cover." The species epithet *cyanellus* is also Greek and means "blue."

Biology: The green sunfish is a very versatile species, able to tolerate a wide range of environmental conditions, and tends to do very well when competition with other sunfish is minimal. Its ability to tolerate environmental extremes makes it ideal for survival in prairie streams where conditions are not stable, and they are often the first sunfish species to repopulate depleted areas. Green sunfish nest in shallow water colonies where nests are often closely packed. Gravel or rocky bottom sites are usually preferred for nest building. Spawning occurs in late spring, when water temperatures rise above 70°F, and may continue throughout the summer. Hybridization with other sunfish species is very common. Males aggressively defend their nests for 6-7 days after eggs are deposited, at which time fry are usually free-swimming. Because of their enormous reproductive potential, green sunfish often overpopulate small lakes and ponds. Adults feed on insects and small fish.

Angling Importance: Due to their propensity to overpopulate and so become stunted, they rarely reach a desirable size for angling. The largest reported specimen taken by rod-and-reel anglers in Texas to date was only 0.75 pounds. However, researchers have reported individuals twice that size.

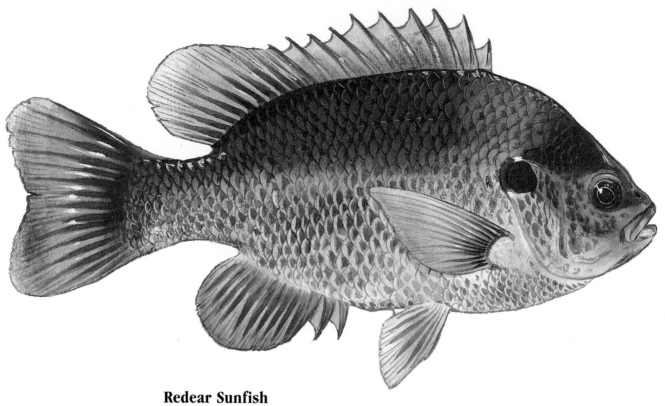

Redear Sunfish
Lepomis microlophus (Cuvier)

Other Names: Shellcracker, Georgia bream, cherry gill, sunny, sun perch

Redear Sunfish—*Lepomis microlophus* (Cuvier)

Distribution: Originally redear sunfish were found in the southeastern U.S. from Texas, north to a line even with southern Illinois, and east to the Atlantic Ocean. As a result of introductions, the range has been expanded and now extends west into New Mexico, and north into Michigan, Ohio and Pennsylvania. In Texas the species is native to the eastern two-thirds of the state from the Red River to the Rio Grande. It has been widely introduced throughout the state.

Description: *Lepomis*, the generic name, is Greek and means "scaled gill cover," and the species epithet *microlophus* is Greek for "small nape." The redear is a deep-bodied sunfish, with a relatively small mouth. Color ranges from dark olive green above to almost white on the belly. The sides are usually yellow to green. The spinous dorsal fin, which is anterior to the soft dorsal fin, is normally equipped with 10 spines, although 9 or 11 spines are sometimes observed, and it is broadly connected to the soft dorsal fin. The anal fin has three spines. The species' most distinct characteristic is the red edge on the opercle ("ear") flap of the male (orange on the female). The opercle flap is never greatly elongated as in some other similar species such as the redbreast sunfish *Lepomis auritus* or the longear sunfish *Lepomis megalotis*.

Biology: Redear sunfish often utilize snails as a major food item, hence the common name "shellcracker." However, insect larvae and cladocerans (see glossary) may also be found in their diet. The species is usually found near the bottom in warm water with little current and abundant aquatic vegetation. Redear sunfish normally reach sexual maturity by the end of their second year. They generally spawn during the warm months of late spring and early summer, and in deeper water than most other sunfish, congregating in spawning "beds." Nests are saucer-shaped depressions in gravel or silt, and are sometimes so close they almost touch. There are usually one or two peaks of activity during spawning season. Few survive more than six summers.

Angling Importance: Unlike some other sunfish species, redears rarely approach the surface to take flies or other artificial top baits. They may, however, be readily captured using natural bait such as earthworms and grubs. Redear are often taken in early summer when they are concentrated on spawning beds.

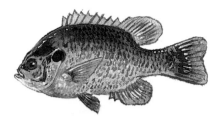

Colors of breeding male are intense, showy

Colors fade soon after redear is caught

Longear Sunfish—*Lepomis megalotis* (Rafinesque)

Longear Sunfish
Lepomis megalotis (Rafinesque)

Other Names: Cherry bream, sunny, sun perch

Longear Sunfish—*Lepomis megalotis* (Rafinesque)

Distribution: Longear sunfish are restricted to freshwater areas west of the Appalachian Mountains. Scattered populations occur as far north and west as southern Quebec and Minnesota, and as far south and west as north-central Mexico and New Mexico. The species is found throughout Texas, except for the headwaters of the Canadian and Brazos rivers.

Description: *Lepomis*, the generic name, is Greek and means "scaled gill cover;" the species epithet *megalotis* is also Greek and means "great ear." The name is derived from the fact that longear sunfish have an elongated opercle flap. This elongated flap, which is always trimmed in white in adults, is unique and makes field identification relatively easy (assuming hybridization has not occurred). Longear sunfish are quite colorful. Males are often bright orange or scarlet, and the head and fins usually have turquoise markings. Dorsal and anal fins, and their associated spines, are similar to those of redear sunfish.

Biology: Longear sunfish are primarily found in small streams and creeks. Like other sunfish, they are often associated with vegetation, and avoid strong currents by inhabiting pools, inlets and waters off the main stream channel. Spawning occurs throughout late spring and early summer. Males scoop nests

out of gravel bars. Females are enticed to lay their eggs on a particular nest by a male who swims out to meet her, circling her rapidly, and displaying his brilliant spawning colors. After the eggs have been laid, males chase the females away and guard the nest vigorously, despite their relatively small size, chasing away all intruders. Males may continue to guard the nest for a week or more after hatching, until the larvae have dispersed. Insects and even small fish become part of the diet as fish approach adulthood. Longear sunfish rarely exceed six inches in length.

Angling Importance: Because of its small size, the species' importance to anglers is derived in three ways. First, since these sunfish are relatively easy to capture with simple, natural baits such as earthworms, longears are an important species for young anglers with little experience. Like most sunfish, they provide more than enough fight for their small size. Second, longears may feed on the surface, hence they may provide the fly-fishermen with a challenge, and finally they are often a prized baitfish for trotliners.

Midges are tiny aquatic insects. Eggs, larvae and pupae live in the water, but adults emerge as small flies. Most are non-biting, but they may form swarms. Midge larvae are readily consumed by small fish. The larvae of some species living in or near bottom sediments are called "blood-worms" because of their red color. This color is due to hemoglobin which helps them live in areas where oxygen levels sometime fall very low.

Bluegill—*Lepomis macrochirus* (Rafinesque)

Bluegill
Lepomis macrochirus (Rafinesque)

Other Names: Bream, brim, perch, sunfish, sunny, sun perch

Bluegill—*Lepomis macrochirus* (Rafinesque)

Distribution: Bluegills appear to have been native to the eastern half of the U.S. including south-eastern Canada and northeastern Mexico, exclusive of the coastal plain north of Virginia. Today, as a result of countless intentional as well as no doubt unintentional introductions, the species is found throughout the U.S. and northern Mexico. Three subspecies are present in Texas, *Lepomis macrochirus macrochirus*, native to the northeastern half of the state; *Lepomis macrochirus speciosus*, native to the central, southern and western portions of the state; and *Lepomis macrochirus purpurescens*, a native of Atlantic Coast states which has been introduced widely as a sport and forage fish in Texas.

Description: *Lepomis*, the generic name, is Greek and means "scaled gill cover;" the species epithet *macrochirus* is also Greek and means "large hand" which may refer to the body shape or its size. Bluegills may be distinguished from other sunfish by the dark spot at the rear of the dorsal fin, vertical bars on their sides, and a relatively small mouth. The spiny dorsal fin usually has 10 spines (but may have as many as 11 or as few as 9), and is broadly connected to the soft dorsal. The anal fin has three spines. The back and upper sides are usually dark olive-green blending to lavender, brown, copper or orange on the sides, and

reddish-orange or yellow on the belly. Colors are more intense in breeding males, and vertical bars may take on a reddish hue.

Biology: Bluegills begin spawning when water temperatures reach about 70°F. Spawning may peak in May or June, but continues until water temperatures cool in the fall. Because of their long spawning season, bluegills have very high reproductive potential, which often results in overpopulation when there is low predation or low fishing pressure. Nests are created in shallow water, one to two feet in depth. A gravel substrate is preferred. Fifty or more nests may be crowded into a small area, thus creating a spawning "bed." Males guard the nest until the eggs hatch and fry leave. Young fish feed on plankton, but as they grow the diet shifts to aquatic insects and their larvae. Up to 50% of their diet may consist of midge larvae.

Angling Importance: Although less than one percent of licensed Texas anglers say they "prefer" to catch sunfish, bluegill and other sunfish are nevertheless a vital part of many freshwater fisheries nationwide, including Texas. Many pre-license age anglers begin their fishing careers by bank fishing for bluegills and other sunfish. Bluegills provide plenty of fight, pound for pound. In Texas bluegills

approaching two pounds have been landed in public waters, and fish over three pounds are known from private tanks. The largest bluegill on record was 4 pounds 12 ounces, landed in 1950 from Ketona Lake in Alabama.

Male bluegill, above, is brightly marked in spawning condition while female, below, is duller in color and round with eggs

White Crappie
Pomoxis annularis (Rafinesque)

Other Names: White perch, sac-a-lait

White Crappie—*Pomoxis annularis* (Rafinesque)

Distribution: The native range of white crappie included the area west of the Appalachian Mountains north to southern Ontario and south to the Gulf of Mexico. The range extended west to Minnesota and South Dakota in the north, and northeastern Mexico in the south. Today the range extends east to the Atlantic Coast, and west to include California and portions of Nevada, Arizona, New Mexico, Montana, Colorado, Utah and North Dakota. In Texas white crappie are native to the eastern two-thirds of the state, but the species may now be found statewide except for the upper portions of the Rio Grande and Pecos drainages.

Description: *Pomoxis* is Greek for "opercle sharp," and refers to the fact that this fish's gill covers have spines. The word *annularis* is Latin for "having rings," and refers to the dark bands (vertical bars) around the body. The white crappie is deep-bodied and silvery in color, ranging from silvery white on the belly to a silvery green or even dark green on the back. There are several vertical bars on the sides. The dorsal fin usually has six spines. Males may develop dark coloration in the throat region during the spring spawning season.

Biology: Like other members of the sunfish family white crappie are nest builders. They are similar to bluegills in that they tend to nest in relatively large "beds," and have very high reproductive potential which often leads to overpopulation and stunting in small lakes and impoundments. White crappie nest in the spring, generally when water temperatures reach 65°F to 70°F. However, spawning activity has been observed at temperatures as low as 56°F. Fry hatch in about three to five days, but remain attached to the bottom of the nest by an adhesive substance from the egg, for a few more days. Just before leaving the nest, fry free themselves by vigorous swimming actions. Once free they begin feeding on microscopic animals. Although fry do not appear to school, fingerlings do. Schools are often found with large numbers of individuals in the middle of lakes. Typically, white crappie grow three to five inches in length the first year, and reach seven to eight inches during the second year. Maturity is usually reached in two to three years. Adults feed on small fish and insects.

Angling Importance: Taken together "crappie" (white and black crappie combined) are the most popular panfish in Texas. The "crappie" group is the third most preferred group overall, ranking behind only "bass" and "catfish." Crappie are sought after by both bank and boat anglers. Typically, minnows are the preferred bait, often producing monumental results when an aggregation is located, usually around submerged trees, boat docks, or other submerged structures. White crappie in excess of 4.5 pounds have been landed in Texas waters.

Black Crappie
Pomoxis nigromaculatus (Lesueur)

Other Names: White perch, calico bass

Black Crappie—*Pomoxis nigromaculatus* (Lesueur)

Distribution: The native range of the species was very similar to that of the white crappie, with the exception that it extended slightly further north into Canada, and east to the coastal plain south of Virginia. Currently, populations of black crappie can be found in each of the 48 contiguous United States. In Texas, black crappie are native to the central portions of the state exclusive of the Edwards Plateau, and have been widely introduced. However, black crappie are abundant primarily in clear, acidic waters of east Texas.

Description: *Pomoxis* is Greek for "opercle sharp," and refers to the fact that the gill covers have spines. The species epithet *nigro-maculatus* is Latin and means "black spotted." The black crappie is easily confused with the white crappie. However, it is deeper bodied than its relative and silvery-green in color. There are no distinct vertical bars; rather there are irregular black blotches. The dorsal fin has seven or eight spines. As in white crappie, males may develop dark coloration during the spring spawning season. The species may be misidentified as white perch.

Biology: Again, like other members of the sunfish family, black crappie are nest builders. They nest in spring, generally when water temperatures reach 60°F. The biology of black crappie is very similar to that of white crappie. Growth in terms of weight is very similar between the two species. White crappie tend to have higher growth rates in terms of length, but black crappie are more robust in body construction. Also, adults feed on fewer fish, and more insects and crustaceans than do white crappie.

Angling Importance: Black crappie predominate in Texas' acidic waters of the east and northeast. Texas' public waters have yielded black crappie over 3.5 pounds, and specimens of almost 4.5 pounds have been recorded from private waters.

 Did You Know?

Put-and-take fisheries are those where catchable-sized fish are stocked and harvest is allowed immediately. Often these fisheries are comprised of small urban impoundments and fishing pressure is such that very few stocked fish are left just days or weeks later. Put-grow-and-take fisheries are those where stocked fish are allowed to grow into catchable size.

Striped Bass—*Morone saxatilis* (Walbaum)

Striped Bass
Morone saxatilis (Walbaum)

Other Names: Striper, rockfish, lineside

Striped Bass—*Morone saxatilis* (Walbaum)

Distribution: The striped bass is a coastal species that moves far upstream during spawning migrations in coastal rivers. The native range is along the Atlantic coast east of the Appalachian Mountains from New Brunswick south to Florida and west into Louisiana. The species has been introduced at scattered locations throughout the central and western U.S. Although not native to Texas, the species has been stocked in a number of reservoirs where excellent fisheries are maintained. Most notable is Lake Texoma along the Red River in northeastern Texas.

Description: The striped bass is the largest member of the temperate-bass or "true" bass family, to distinguish them from species such as largemouth, smallmouth and spotted bass which are actually members of the sunfish family Centrarchidae. Although *Morone* is of unknown derivation, *saxatilis* is Latin, meaning "dwelling among rocks." As with other true basses, the dorsal fin is clearly separated into spiny and soft-rayed portions. Striped bass are silvery, shading to olive-green on the back and white on the belly, with seven or eight uninterrupted horizontal stripes on each side of the body. Younger fish may resemble white bass, *Morone chrysops*. However, striped bass have two distinct tooth patches on the back of the tongue, whereas white bass have only one

tooth patch. Similarly, striped bass have two sharp points on each gill cover, and white bass have just one. Additionally, the second spine on the anal fin is about half the length of the third spine in striped bass, and about two-thirds the length of the third spine in white bass.

Biology: The striped bass is anadromous, native to a variety of habitats including shores, bays and estuaries. In coastal populations individuals may ascend streams and travel as much as 100 miles inland to spawn. There are land-locked populations that complete their entire life cycle in freshwater. These, generally, have ascended tributaries of the lakes or reservoirs where they and future generations then spend their lives. Spawning begins in the spring when water temperatures approach 60°F. Typically, one female is accompanied by several males during the actual spawning act. Running water is necessary to keep eggs in motion until hatching. In general, 50 miles or more of stream is required for successful hatches. As a result, with the exceptions of Lake Powell and Lake Texoma, most reservoir populations are not self-sustaining, and must be maintained through stocking. Striped bass "stripers" may reach a size of 10 to 12 inches during the first year. Males are generally mature in two years, and females in three to four. Adults are primarily piscivorous, feeding predominantly

on members of the herring family such as gizzard shad and threadfin shad.

Angling Importance: Striped bass are the fourth most preferred species among licensed Texas anglers. It is estimated that the economic impact of striper fishing in the Lake Texoma area alone totals well in excess of $20 million. Striped bass are often captured using various artificial lures that imitate small fish, such as silver spoons. Deep running lures can also be effective, as may live bait or cut bait. In Texas, striped bass in excess of 45 pounds have been landed. Although specimens exceeding 100 pounds have been caught in saltwater, to date a 66 pounder was the largest individual reported from inland waters.

Hybrid striped bass (striped bass crossbred with white bass) are stocked in many areas because of their quick growth and good survival characteristics. Although the state record is 19.66 pounds, hybrids rarely exceed 10 pounds. Generally, they may be distinguished from white bass in that they typically exceed the maximum size for white bass, and they have two tooth patches in the back of the tongue as opposed to the one in white bass. Hybrids are very similar to striped bass and genetic testing may need to be used to distinguish between them.

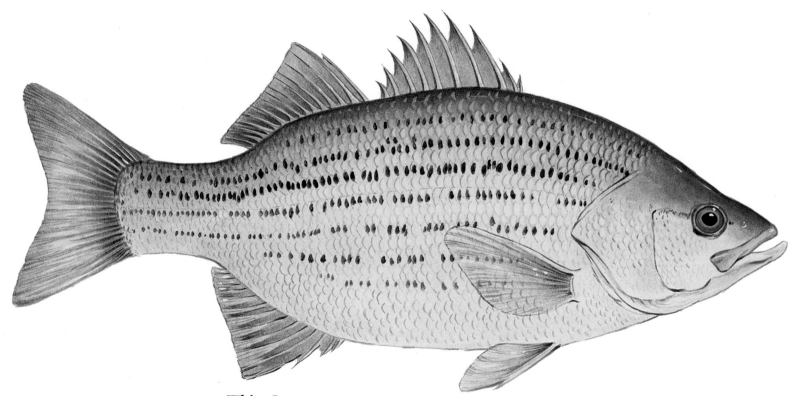

White Bass
Morone chrysops (Rafinesque)

Other Names: Sand bass, barfish, striped bass, striper, streaker, silver bass

White Bass—*Morone chrysops* (Rafinesque)

Distribution: White bass are native to the central U.S. west of the Appalachians, including the Great Lakes, as well as river systems in the Ohio and Mississippi river valleys. The species' native range extended south and west as far as Texas, including the Rio Grande and Red River drainages.

Description: *Morone* is of unknown derivation; however, *chrysops* is Greek meaning "golden eye." Again, as with other true basses, the dorsal fin is clearly double, separated into spiny and soft-rayed portions. White bass are silvery, shading from dark-gray or black on the back to white on the belly. Several incomplete lines or stripes run horizontally on each side of the body. Adults resemble young striped bass, and the two are often confused. However, striped bass have two distinct tooth patches on the back of the tongue, and white bass have only one tooth patch. Similarly, striped bass have two sharp points on each gill cover, as opposed to white bass which have one. Also, the second spine on the anal fin is about half the length of the third spine in striped bass, whereas it is about two-thirds the length of the third spine in white bass.

Biology: White bass are active early spring spawners. Schools of males migrate upstream to spawning areas as much as a month before females. There is no nest preparation. Spawning occurs either near the surface, or in midwater. Running water with a gravel or rock substrate is preferred. Females rise to the surface and several males crowd around as the eggs and sperm are released. Large females sometimes release nearly a million small eggs during the spawning season. After release, eggs sink to the bottom and become attached to rocks, hatching in 2–3 days. Fry grow rapidly, feeding on small invertebrates. White bass may grow eight or nine inches during the first year. Adults are usually found in schools. Feeding occurs near the surface where fish, crustaceans and emerging insects are found in abundance. Gizzard and threadfin shad are the preferred food items. White bass greater than four years of age are rare.

Angling Importance: White bass are the fifth most preferred species among licensed Texas anglers. Schools of white bass feeding on shad generate much excitement among anglers. Once a school has been located, successful anglers often fish the surface with spoons or spinners. Alternatively, bottom fishing at night with live bait may also produce great success. White bass are excellent fighters, and are considered superb table fare.

A relationship between the number of eggs produced and **recruitment** (number of fish "recruited" to the fishery by reaching a size large enough to be legally harvested) is often very difficult to find since many factors strongly affect the growth and survival of young fish.

Yellow Bass—*Morone mississippiensis* (Jordan and Eigenmann)

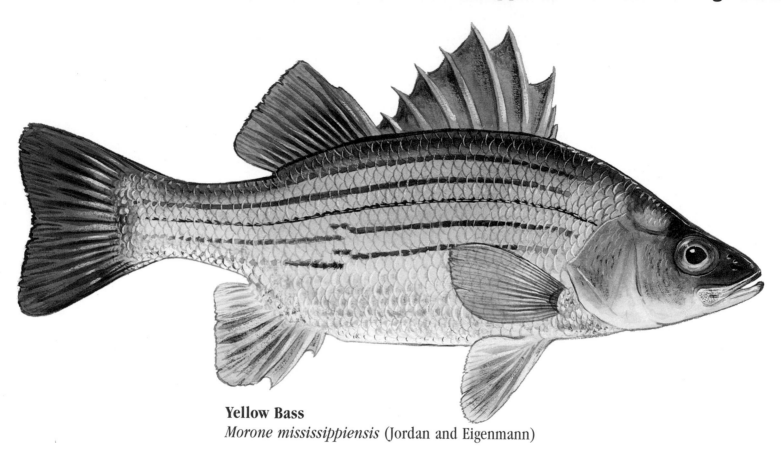

Yellow Bass
Morone mississippiensis (Jordan and Eigenmann)

Other Names: Striper

Yellow Bass—*Morone mississippiensis* (Jordan and Eigenmann)

Distribution: Although native populations do exist in areas of Oklahoma, Texas and Mississippi, the species was primarily restricted to the Mississippi River from Minnesota to Louisiana. Introduced populations occur as far west as Arizona, as far north as Wisconsin and Iowa, and as far east as central Tennessee. In east Texas yellow bass range from the Red River south to the San Jacinto drainage.

Description: The meaning of the word *Morone* is unknown; *mississippiensis* refers to the Mississippi River from which the species was first described. Although yellow bass are sometimes confused with white bass or young striped bass, there are several distinguishing characteristics. First, the belly and/or sides may take on a yellow color from which the species derives its common name. Second, unlike other temperate bass, the two lower-most stripes are distinctively broken just posterior to the middle, and third, the second and third anal spines are approximately equal in length.

Biology: Yellow bass, like other members of the temperate-bass family are spring spawners. They prefer gravel or rock substrate for spawning, but unlike other temperate basses they do not appear to require flowing water, and they temporarily pair during spawning. Eggs are usually deposited in two to three feet of water. At water temperatures of 70°F eggs hatch in four to six days. Yellow bass are slow growers, reaching four or five inches the first year, and only growing one to two inches per year thereafter. They reach sexual maturity in only two years (six to seven inches). Young fish feed primarily on fish, crustaceans and insects. Adults often eat large quantities of fish, and may even cannibalize their own young. Schools are most often found in midwater or near the surface.

Angling Importance: Yellow bass are often found in schools. Like white bass they may be captured using spoons, spinners or live minnows. However, due to their small size, averaging only about half a pound, and slow growth rate they are not highly sought by most anglers (a trophy fish may not exceed one pound).

At spawning time, gold is more pronounced in the male shown opposite, while both sexes are less showy in color summer and winter, above

Rio Grande Cichlid—*Cichlasoma cyanoguttatum* (Baird and Girard)

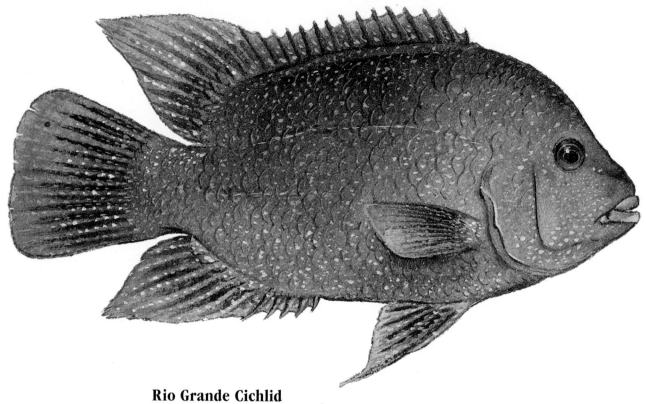

Rio Grande Cichlid

Cichlasoma cyanoguttatum (Baird and Girard)

Other Names: Rio Grande perch, Texas cichlid

Rio Grande Cichlid—*Cichlasoma cyanoguttatum* (Baird and Girard)

Distribution: The distribution of the Rio Grande cichlid in Texas appears to have originally been limited to the lower reaches of the Rio Grande. However, a number of populations have been established in large springs and rivers of Central Texas' Edwards Plateau including the San Marcos, Guadalupe, San Antonio and Colorado rivers. Minimum temperature tolerances in the Colorado River have been measured at 57–66°F.

Description: *Cichlasoma* is derived from the Greek word for "thrush" *cichla*, and means "resembling cichla." The word *cyanoguttatum* is also Greek and means "blue spotted." Rio Grande cichlids are distinctive in that they exhibit cream and turquoise colored spots giving them a speckled look. Background color varies from very dark to light olive. Lighter colored specimens usually exhibit five dark vertical bars. Both dorsal and anal fins are long and tapered extending behind the caudal peduncle (fleshy portion of the tail). Unlike tilapia, and most sunfishes, which typically have three spines on the anal fin, Rio Grande cichlids are equipped with five to six anal fin spines. Adult males may also develop a pronounced "hump" on the head which is not present in tilapia. Adults usually range up to about 6 inches in length.

Biology: Like most of their family, Rio Grande cichlids are generally considered warm-water fish, and are very sensitive to cold water temperatures. In general, Rio Grande cichlids do not survive at water temperatures below 49°F. The species may do well in heated water, and in spring-fed waters with constant favorable temperatures. Spawning occurs in early spring. Both parents protect their young, which feed primarily on small fish, insects and crustaceans. Adults are also known to consume large quantities of fish eggs when they are available.

Angling Importance: Rio Grande cichlids are fine fighters, and easily caught. They are considered good table fare. The Texas state record was caught in Lake Dunlap in 1994 and weighed just under one pound.

In warm, clear water this cichlid has conspicuous bars with cream and turquoise spots, above, while cooler waters produce grey coloration, below

This species pales from stress of capture, above

Blue Tilapia
Tilapia aurea (Steindachner)

Other Names: Tilapia, tilapia-perch, Nile perch

Blue Tilapia—*Tilapia aurea* (Steindachner)

Distribution: Tilapia were originally distributed throughout a wide band of sub-Saharan Africa, with several isolated populations in east Africa. Currently, in North America there are established populations in Texas, Florida, and possibly Arizona, Georgia and Colorado. In Texas, established populations exist in the Rio Grande, San Antonio, Guadalupe and Colorado River drainages. Blue tilapia are usually able to establish populations in areas without extremely cold winter temperatures, since their lower temperature tolerance is about 55°F. They are able to live and reproduce in both fresh and brackish water.

Description: *Tilapia* is a Latinized version of the African name for this fish, and *aurea* is Latin for "gold" or "yellow." Apparently Steindachner was working with a preserved specimen when the fish was named, and the preservative had turned the fish yellow. Typically, live specimens are silvery-grey in color, and deep-bodied. Both the dorsal and caudal fins are edged in red. Blue tilapia may be readily distinguished from Rio Grande cichlids in that they generally have three, rather than five or six, anal fin spines.

Biology: Blue tilapia construct nests during spawning. Unfortunately, their vigorous nest digging often disturbs the spawning activities of native fish species, such as largemouth bass. The eggs are almost immediately taken up into the females mouth where they are incubated (making them functional mouth brooders). They are mature at about seven-and-one-half inches, may reach 17 inches in Texas, and usually do not exceed five pounds in weight. Blue tilapia are omnivorous. They are fond of filamentous algae, but may also utilize phytoplankton, vascular plants and invertebrates. Occasionally they eat small fish. Typically, they tend to overpopulate, especially in small lakes and ponds.

Angling Importance: Blue tilapia are of negligible importance as a sport species. They rarely take any bait, natural or artificial. However, an occasional fish is taken. The state record to date for rod and reel angling is just over five pounds.

Since **tilapia** generally require water in excess of about 55°F, these fish are most likely to survive Texas winters in power plant reservoirs where temperatures are artificially raised by water used for cooling.

Flathead Catfish
Pylodictis olivaris (Rafinesque)

Other Names: Yellow cat, opelousas, mud cat, shovelhead cat, goujon, appaluchion, johnnie cat

Flathead Catfish—*Pylodictis olivaris* (Rafinesque)

Distribution: The native range includes a broad area west of the Appalachian Mountains encompassing large rivers of the Mississippi, Missouri and Ohio basins. The range extends as far north as North Dakota, as far west as New Mexico, and south to the Gulf including eastern Mexico. Flathead catfish occur statewide in Texas.

Description: *Pylodictis* is Greek, meaning "mud fish," and *olivaris* is Latin for "olive-colored." Flathead catfish are typically pale yellow (hence the name "yellow cat") to light brown on the back and sides, and highly mottled with black and/or brown. The belly is usually pale yellow or cream colored. The head is broadly flattened, with a projecting lower jaw. The tail fin is only slightly notched, not deeply forked as is the case with blue and channel catfish. Young fish may be very dark, almost black in appearance.

Biology: In Texas flathead catfish may spawn from late May through August. Males construct nests by excavating a shallow depression in a natural cavity (such as hollow logs, caves or crevices), or near a large object. Females are encouraged to lay their eggs in the nest by males. Over 100,000 eggs may be found in a golden-yellow egg mass which is guarded viciously by the male. Young generally hatch in four to six days. They may school together for several days near the nest, but soon disperse and seek shelter under rocks or brush. Fingerlings feed on insect larvae, juveniles feed on small fish and crayfish, while adults feed almost exclusively on fish, indeed more so than other catfishes. Adults are usually solitary, each staking out a favorite spot, typically in deeper water or under cover, during the day. At night they may move into riffles and shallow areas to feed.

Angling Importance: The flathead catfish is the second largest freshwater sportfish in Texas, being outmuscled only by the blue catfish. Where mature populations exist, 50-pounders are not unusual. Typically, the largest fish are caught by trotliners, some of whom have landed specimens in excess of 110 pounds. "Catfish" is the second most preferred group of fish by licensed Texas anglers, and flatheads rank second behind channel catfish. Rod-and-reel anglers may have the greatest success with flathead catfish just below reservoir dams.

Black Bullhead
Ameiurus melas (Rafinesque)

Other Names: Polliwog, chucklehead cat, mud cat

Black Bullhead—*Ameiurus melas* (Rafinesque)

Distribution: The original distribution of the black bullhead included the central plains west of the Appalachians and east of the Rockies, extending north into Saskatchewan and Manitoba, and south into south Texas and New Mexico. Today artificial introductions have extended the range west of the Rockies in isolated pockets, including areas of British Columbia, Alberta, Mexico, California, Arizona, Nevada and Idaho. In Texas the black bullhead is distributed statewide with the exception of the Trans-Pecos drainage.

Description: *Ameiurus* is Greek and means "primitive or curtailed" in reference to the slight notch in the caudal fin; *melas* is also Greek and means "black." Black bullheads are typically black to greenish-black on the back, ranging to gray or white on the belly. However, in muddy water the back may be yellowish-brown. Chin barbels are dark or black, never white. The anal fin has 17–21 rays.

Biology: During late spring or early summer black bullheads excavate nests in mud bottoms and spawn. Areas with some sort of cover are preferred. Nests contain golden-yellow egg masses which are guarded by both parents (at least one is present at all times). In four to six days eggs hatch and fry begin to school in compact balls which are guarded by adults until individuals reach about one inch in length. Black bullheads are omnivorous, feeding primarily from the bottom on a wide range of plant and animal material, both live and dead. Fingerlings feed almost exclusively on crustaceans. Immature aquatic insects and crustaceans often comprise a considerable proportion of the adult diet. The average life span is usually less than five years, and most adults are less than one pound. However, some individuals may live more than 10 years and reach eight pounds.

Angling Importance: Black bullheads are not generally considered an important gamefish in Texas, although they are readily fished for by anglers in the Panhandle and in far east Texas. A variety of baits may be used to catch them, but worms are usually the best. The largest specimen reported to date in Texas was 4.53 pounds.

Yellow Bullhead
Ameiurus natalis (Lesueur)

Other Names: Polliwog, chucklehead cat, yellow cat

Yellow Bullhead—*Ameiurus natalis* (Lesueur)

Distribution: Yellow bullheads range through-out the central and eastern U.S., from central Texas north into North Dakota and east through the Great Lakes region to the coast. The species is found throughout Texas with the exclusion of the Trans-Pecos and Panhandle regions.

Description: *Ameiurus* means "primitive or curtailed" in reference to the notch in the distal end of the caudal fin, and *natalis* is Latin for "having large buttocks." Yellow bull-heads are typically light yellow to olive-green on the back, often somewhat mottled. The belly is yellowish to white. The tail is not notched, and may be slightly rounded. Chin barbels are white. The anal fin has 23–27 rays.

Biology: During late spring or early summer yellow bullheads excavate nests in mud bottoms and spawn. Both parents guard the nest, which may contain 2,000 to 12,000 eggs. In four to six days eggs hatch and fry begin to school in compact balls which are guarded by adults until individuals reach about one inch in length. Like black bullheads, the yellow bull-head is omnivorous, feeding on a variety of plant and animal material, both live and dead. Immature aquatic insects and crustaceans often comprise a considerable proportion of the diet.

Although yellow bullheads rarely achieve edible size, some individuals may exceed four pounds.

Angling Importance: Like black bullheads, yellow bullheads are not generally considered an important gamefish in Texas. But again, as with the black bullhead, anglers in the Panhandle and in far east Texas often fish for yellow bullheads. Angling techniques for the two species are very similar. The largest specimen reported to date in Texas was 5.59 pounds.

Water hyacinth is a floating aquatic plant, native to South America, that has been called the world's worst weed. It may form large floating mats that shade the growth of submerged plants important to fish communi-ties, and inhibit boat traffic and other recreation on infested water bodies.

Channel Catfish—*Ictalurus punctatus* (Rafinesque)

Channel Catfish
Ictalurus punctatus (Rafinesque)

Other Names: Willow cat, forked-tail cat, fiddler, spotted cat, lady cat

Channel Catfish—*Ictalurus punctatus* (Rafinesque)

Distribution: Channel catfish are native to North America east of the Rockies from southern Canada, south into northeastern Mexico, and east of the Appalachians with the exception of much of the coastal plain north of Florida. The species has been widely introduced in other areas as far west as California. Today channel catfish range throughout Texas; however, it is believed that the species was not native to the upper Rio Grande and Pecos basins.

Description: *Ictalurus* is Greek, and *punctatus* is Latin, meaning "fish cat" and "spotted," respectively. Although channel catfish are often mistaken for blue catfish, they are easily distinguished from all other catfish species in Texas by their deeply forked tail fin. Unlike flathead catfish, the upper jaw projects beyond the lower jaw. Coloration is olive-brown to slate-blue on the back and sides, shading to silvery-white on the belly. Typically, numerous small irregular, black spots are present, but may be obscured in large adults. The anal fin has a curved margin and 24–29 soft rays, as opposed to the blue catfish anal fin which has a straight margin and 30 or more rays.

Biology: Channel catfish may be abundant in reservoirs, and in large streams with low or moderate current. They spawn in late spring or early summer when water temperatures reach 75°F. Males select nest sites which are normally dark secluded areas such as cavities in drift piles, logs, undercut banks, rocks, cans, etc. A golden-yellow gelatinous egg mass is deposited in the bottom of the nest. Males guard the nest, and may actually eat some of the eggs if they are disturbed. The eggs, if not devoured, typically hatch in about a week. Fry remain in the nest, under the guardianship of the male, for about another week. Young fish appear to be most susceptible to predation in clear water where survival during the first year of life is much lower than under turbid conditions. Channel catfish less than 4 inches in length feed primarily on small insects. Adults are largely omnivorous, feeding on insects, mollusks, crustaceans, fish and even some plant material. Sexual maturity is reached in two or three years in captivity, whereas data from natural populations indicates channel catfish in Texas reach sexual maturity in 3–6 years. Most are mature by the time they reach 12 inches in length.

Angling Importance: Channel catfish rank behind only bass and crappie as the most preferred fish to catch in Texas. Popular among trotliners, as well as rod-and-reel anglers, channel catfish may be captured on a wide variety of baits, including liver, worms, grasshoppers, shrimp, chicken, cheese and stink bait among others. Undoubtedly, part of the reason for their popularity is their delicious flavor when cooked, as evidenced by the fact that they are raised commercially for consumption. Channel catfish in excess of 36 pounds have been landed in Texas waters. The North American record now stands at 58 pounds.

Blue Catfish
Ictalurus furcatus (Lesueur)

Other Names: Hump-backed blue, white cat, silver cat, blue fulton, white fulton, blue channel cat, high-fin blue, government blue

Blue Catfish—*Ictalurus furcatus* (Lesueur)

Distribution: Blue catfish are native to major rivers of the Ohio, Missouri and Mississippi river basins. The range also extends south through Texas, Mexico and into northern Guatemala. In Texas it is absent from the northwestern portions of the state including the Panhandle, but present elsewhere in larger rivers.

Description: *Ictalurus* is Greek, meaning "fish cat," and *furcatus* is Latin, meaning "forked," a reference to the species' forked tail fin. Unlike channel catfish, blue catfish generally are not spotted — only the Rio Grande population has dark spots on the back and sides — being usually an even slate-blue on the back, shading to white on the belly. Also the number of rays in the anal fin is higher, typically from 30–35.

Biology: Blue catfish are primarily a large-river fish, occurring in main channels, tributaries and impoundments of major river systems. They may tend to move upstream in the summer in search of cooler temperatures, and downstream in the winter in order to find warmer water. Their spawning behavior appears to be similar to that of channel catfish. However, most blue catfish are not sexually mature until they reach about 24 inches in length. Like channel catfish, the blue catfish diet is quite varied, but with a tendency to eat fish earlier in life. Although invertebrates still comprise the major portion of the diet, blue catfish as small as four inches in length have been known to consume fish. Individuals larger than eight inches eat fish and large invertebrates. Blue catfish commonly attain weights of 20–40 pounds, and may reach weights well in excess of 100 pounds. It is reported that fish exceeding 350 pounds were landed from the Mississippi River during the late 1800s.

Angling Importance: The blue catfish is the largest freshwater sportfish in Texas. Where mature populations exist, 50-pounders are not unusual. Typically, the largest fish are caught by trotliners, some of whom have landed specimens in excess of 115 pounds. "Catfish" is the second most preferred group of fish by licensed Texas anglers, and blues rank third behind channel catfish and flathead catfish. Rod-and-reel anglers have landed specimens in excess of 80 pounds. Like the channel catfish, the blue catfish is considered an excellent food as well as sportfish.

Most fish species undergo various critical periods in their life cycles during which **survival** hangs in the balance, and may be subject to the vagaries of weather, or the presence of other species. One such period is just after the yolk-sac is absorbed. If the proper food isn't immediately available, mortality may be very high due to starvation. On the other hand, if conditions are just right to provide needed food organisms, survival tends to be high, resulting in a strong year class.

Alligator gar—*Lepisosteus spatula* (Lacépède)

Alligator gar
Lepisosteus spatula (Lacépède)

Other Names: Gator gar

Alligator gar—*Lepisosteus spatula* (Lacépède)

Distribution: Alligator gar are present in the Gulf Coastal Plain from the Econfina River in west Florida west and south to Veracruz, Mexico. The species range extends north in the Mississippi River basin to the lower reaches of the Missouri and Ohio rivers. An isolated population also occurs in Nicaragua. In Texas alligator gar may be found in coastal rivers and streams from the Red River down to the Rio Grande.

Description: Gars are easily distinguished from other freshwater species by their long, slender, cylindrical bodies, their long snouts, and by the fact that they are equipped with diamond-shaped interlocking bony (ganoid) scales. Additionally, the dorsal and anal fins are placed well back on the body, and nearly opposite each other. The tail fin is rounded. Alligator gar may be distinguished from other gars by the presence of two rows of large teeth on either side of the upper jaw in large young and adults. Coloration is generally brown or olive above, and lighter underneath. *Lepisosteus* is Greek, meaning "bony scale," and *spatula* is Latin for "spoon," referring to the creatures broad snout.

Biology: Little is known about the biology of this huge fish. They appear to spawn in the spring beginning sometime in May. Eggs are deposited in shallow water. Alligator gar are usually found in slow sluggish waters, although running water seems to be necessary for spawning. Young fish may consume insects. Adults feed primarily on fish, but will also take waterfowl. The species is able to tolerate greater salinities than other gar species and feeds heavily on marine catfish when those are available.

Angling Importance: Gar have traditionally been considered rough fish by the majority of anglers. However, for a relatively few mavericks, gar fishing is quite an exciting and enjoyable sport. In Texas, alligator gar up to 279 pounds have been captured by rod-and-reel anglers, and trotliners record catches of over 300 pounds. In the southeastern part of the state, gar is commonly accepted as a fine food fish. Alligator gar are often taken by anglers using nylon threads, rather than hooks, to entangle the fish's many sharp teeth, or by bowfishing.

Shortnose Gar—*Lepisosteus platostomus* (Rafinesque)

Shortnose Gar

Lepisosteus platostomus (Rafinesque)

Other Names: Billy gar, short-billed gar, stub-nose gar

Shortnose Gar—*Lepisosteus platostomus* (Rafinesque)

Distribution: Shortnose gar are present in the Mississippi River drainage from the Gulf Coast as far north as Montana in the west, and the Ohio River in the east. In Texas shortnose gar may be found in the Red River basin below Lake Texoma.

Description: *Lepisosteus* is Greek, meaning "bony scale," and *platostomus* is also Greek, meaning "broad mouth." Shortnose gar may be distinguished from other Texas species in that they lack the double row of teeth in the upper jaw of the alligator gar, the long snout of the longnose gar, and the spots of the spotted gar.

Biology: Shortnose gar spawning activity may occur from May into July. Females are often accompanied by more than one male. Yellow eggs are scattered in vegetation and other submerged structures, usually hatching within eight days of spawning. The fry remain in the yolk-sac phase for another week, at which time they begin to feed on insect larvae and small crustaceans. At little over an inch in length, fish appear in the diet. Sexual maturity is usually achieved when fish reach about 15 inches in length. Shortnose gar are more tolerant of high turbidity than other gar species. Shortnose gar inhabit large rivers and their backwaters, as well as oxbow lakes and large pools.

Angling Importance: As with alligator gar, shortnose gar may be captured by entangling the teeth in nylon threads, or by bowfishing. Shortnose gar up to five pounds have been brought in by anglers. There is no state record reported for shortnose gar in Texas. However, the world all-tackle record stands at five pounds.

Spotted Gar
Lepisosteus oculatus (Winchell)

Other Names: None

Spotted Gar—*Lepisosteus oculatus* [Winchell]

Distribution: Spotted gar are found from central Texas east into western Florida. The species range extends north through the Mississippi River drainage into Illinois, and the lower Ohio River. Populations also occur in the Lake Erie drainage.

Description: *Lepisosteus* is Greek, meaning "bony scale," and *oculatus* is Latin, meaning "provided with eyes." This last is probably a reference to the many dark spots on the head and body. Spotted gar may be distinguished from other Texas species by the dark roundish spots on the top of the head, the pectoral fins and on the pelvic fins.

Biology: Spawning activity occurs as early as April; in flowing water. Fry feed primarily on insect larvae and small crustaceans. As with other gar species, fish appear in the diet very early. Adult diets may be comprised of over 90% fish. Spotted gar are less tolerant of turbidity than shortnose gar. They are typically associated with aquatic vegetation, or timber, in clear water.

Angling Importance: As with other gar species, spotted gar may be captured by entangling the teeth in nylon threads, or by bowfishing. In Texas, bowfishers have landed spotted gar up to 15 pounds.

Diversity is a term often used in ecology. Although the number of species in a community contribute to its diversity, the term actually has two major components. One is species richness (the total number of species present) and the other is **equitability** (the evenness with which numbers are distributed among species). For example, one would normally think of a community with 10 species as more diverse than one with only five species, if that were the only information available. However, if individuals are evenly distributed among species in the community with five, but in the community with 10 species, 99% of the individuals are from a single species, the community with five species would be considered more diverse.

Longnose Gar—*Lepisosteus osseus* (Linnaeus)

Longnose Gar
Lepisosteus osseus (Linnaeus)

Other Names: Needlenose gar, billfish, billy gar

Longnose Gar—*Lepisosteus osseus* (Linnaeus)

Distribution: Longnose gar range widely throughout the eastern U.S. and north into southern Quebec. The species is especially common in the Mississippi River drainage and in the Carolinas. They may be found as far south and west as the Rio Grande drainage in Mexico, Texas and New Mexico. Longnose gar appear in most Texas rivers.

Description: *Lepisosteus* is Greek, meaning "bony scale," and *osseus* is Latin, meaning "of bone." Longnose gar are distinguished from other gar species found in Texas by the long snout whose length is at least 10 times the minimum width.

Biology: Spawning activity occurs as early as April, in shallow riffle areas. Females, typically the larger sex, may be accompanied by one or many males. Although nests are not prepared, gravel is swept somewhat by the spawning action itself. Each female may deposit a portion of her eggs at several different locations. The adhesive eggs are mixed in the gravel. They hatch in six to eight days. Yolk-sac fry have an adhesive disc on their snouts by which they attach themselves to submerged objects until the yolk sac is absorbed. Fry feed primarily on insect larvae, and small crustaceans such as water fleas. Fish appear in the diet very early. Longnose gar are typically associated with backwaters, low inflow pools and moderately clear streams and often do very well in man-made impoundments.

Angling Importance: Longnose gar may be captured by entangling the teeth in nylon threads, or by bowfishing. In Texas, longnose gar in excess of 80 pounds have been landed using a bow and arrow.

Smallmouth Buffalo—*Ictiobus bubalus* (Rafinesque)

Smallmouth Buffalo
Ictiobus bubalus (Rafinesque)

Other Names: Roach-back, razor-backed buffalo, hump-backed buffalo, liner, blue pancake

Smallmouth Buffalo—*Ictiobus bubalus* [Rafinesque]

Distribution: The native range of the small-mouth buffalo includes larger tributaries of the Mississippi River from Montana east to Pennsylvania and West Virginia. The species is also found in Gulf slope drainages from Alabama to the Rio Grande drainage. In Texas smallmouth buffalo are found in most large streams, rivers and reservoirs exclusive of the Panhandle.

Description: *Ictiobus* and *bubalus* are both Greek words meaning "bull fish" and "buffalo," respectively. The back and sides are light brown or otherwise dark with a coppery or greenish tint. The belly is pale yellow to white. Smallmouth buffalo scales are large, and the species sometimes may be confused with common carp by the novice. However, buffalo lack the barbels of carp. Smallmouth buffalo, as opposed to bigmouth buffalo, have a distinctive "sucker" type mouth, oriented downward.

Biology: Although the life history of small-mouth buffalo is not well understood, spawning seems to occur in the spring when water temperatures reach 60–65°F. Eggs are broadcast over weeds and mud bottom, hatching in one to two weeks. This species is primarily bottom feeding which is why insect larvae, algae, detritus and sand often make up significant portions of the gut contents of this fish.

In Texas, smallmouth buffalo have been known to reach almost 100 pounds.

Angling Importance: Although some anglers consider smallmouth buffalo to be a rough fish, in many areas the species is highly prized. Smallmouth buffalo in excess of 82 pounds have been landed by rod-and-reel anglers, whereas the trotline record is 97 pounds in Texas. Buffalo will sometimes take doughballs made with cottonseed meal, and when hooked provide exceptional sport. Many people may be unaware that smallmouth buffalo are quite a food fish. This is the number one species sold by commercial freshwater fishermen.

Bigmouth Buffalo—*Ictiobus cyprinellus* (Valenciennes)

Bigmouth Buffalo
Ictiobus cyprinellus (Valenciennes)

Other Names: Gourdhead, redmouth buffalo, common buffalo

Bigmouth Buffalo—*Ictiobus cyprinellus* (Valenciennes)

Distribution: Bigmouth buffalo are found in the Lake Erie drainage, and in the Mississippi River drainages from southern Canada south to the Gulf Coast. In Texas the range of the bigmouth buffalo is limited to the Red River below Lake Texoma and to the Sulphur River in the northeast.

Description: *Ictiobus* is Greek for "bull fish," and *cyprinellus* is Latin, meaning "small carp." Bigmouth buffalo are similar in color and shape to smallmouth buffalo, except that the mouth is not oriented downward in typical sucker fashion, but rather straight ahead.

Biology: As with smallmouth buffalo, bigmouth buffalo appear to spawn in very shallow water during the spring when water temperatures reach 60° to 65°F. Eggs hatch in 9–10 days. Typically, the species may occur in schools. Young fish seem to prefer bottom-dwelling invertebrates, while older individuals prefer crustaceans dwelling in the midwater.

Angling Importance: As with smallmouth buffalo, some anglers consider bigmouth buffalo to be a rough fish. However, in many areas the species is highly prized. Bigmouth buffalo in excess of 58 pounds have been landed by rod-and-reel anglers, whereas the trotline record is 75 pounds in Texas. Angling techniques are similar to those used for smallmouth buffalo. Many people consider bigmouth buffalo quite a food fish despite the many bones. Some even relish the species' bony nature.

Did You Know?

In freshwater, fish movement may be studied using surgically implanted radio transmitters. However, since dissolved salts interfere with radio transmission, only tags emitting ultrasonic signals can be used in brackish water and seawater.

Freshwater Drum—*Aplodinotus grunniens* (Rafinesque)

Freshwater Drum
Aplodinotus grunniens (Rafinesque)

Other Names: Drum fish, gaspergou, gou, sheepshead, croaker, white perch, rock perch, silver bass

Freshwater Drum—*Aplodinotus grunniens* (Rafinesque)

Distribution: Freshwater drum occur in a variety of habitats, and are one of the most wide-ranging fish latitudinally in North America. Populations can be found from Hudson Bay in the north to Guatemala in the south. East to west the species ranges from the western slopes of the Appalachians to the eastern slopes of the Rockies. In Texas freshwater drum are ubiquitous, exclusive of the Panhandle.

Description: *Aplodinotus* is Greek for "single back," and *grunniens* is Latin, meaning "grunting," referring to the fact that the species may be observed (or felt) making "grunting" sounds. Except for color, freshwater drum resemble their marine relative, the red drum. They are deep-bodied, and equipped with a long dorsal fin divided into two sections. The dorsal fin usually has 10 spines and 29–32 rays. Freshwater drum are silvery in color and lack the distinctive tail-fin spot of red drum.

Biology: In Texas freshwater drum may spawn in April or May. Spawning seems to occur in open water. The eggs float until they hatch. Freshwater drum appear to spend most of their time at or near the bottom. They feed primarily on fish, crayfish and immature insects, often by rooting around in the substrate or moving rocks to dislodge their prey. The presence of heavy throat-teeth also allows them to consume mollusks. For example, in Lake Erie they have been found feeding on zebra mussels (although not nearly enough to control the zebra mussel population).

Angling Importance: Although freshwater drum are considered rough fish by many anglers, they are prized as food fish in some areas. They are also sought after as bait for other species. In Texas the rod-and-reel record exceeds 30 pounds, and the trotline record is 55 pounds.

Many anglers don't realize that **hooking mortality** (death of fish due to the stress and injury associated with capture and release) is often not immediately apparent. A stressed-out fish may swim away looking quite healthy, but die one to several days later. That is why careful scientific studies rather than personal observation are necessary to determine hooking mortality accurately.

Common Carp
Cyprinus carpio (Linnaeus)

Other Names: German carp, European carp, sewer trout

Common Carp—*Cyprinus carpio* (Linnaeus)

Distribution: Common carp are native to temperate portions of Europe and Asia. They were first introduced into North America in 1877. At that time they were considered so valuable that the precious brood stock was fenced and guarded. Since that time countless introductions both intentional and unintentional have allowed *Cyprinus carpio* to become one of the most widely distributed fish species in North America, ranging from central Canada to central Mexico, and from coast to coast. In Texas, common carp are found statewide.

Description: *Cyprinus* is Greek, and *carpio* is Latin; both words mean "carp." The common carp is a heavy-bodied minnow with barbels on either side of the upper jaw. Typically, color varies from brassy green or yellow, to golden brown, or even silvery. The belly is usually yellowish-white. The dorsal fin with 17–21 rays and the anal fin both have a heavy-toothed spine. Individuals 12–25 inches in length and weighing up to 8–10 pounds are common, although they can grow much larger. Common carp may live in excess of 47 years, and weigh over 75 pounds (The all-tackle world record was landed in 1987 from Lac de St. Cassien, France, and weighed in at 75 pounds 11 ounces.).

Biology: Carp were originally native to Asia. Several hundred years ago they were brought to Europe as a food fish, and in the late 1800s they were introduced to North America where they have become nearly ubiquitous. Carp are primarily a warm-water species, and do very well in warm, muddy, highly productive (eutrophic) waters. Adults spawn in very shallow water in the spring. Eggs are indiscriminately released and hatch in about a week. Fry are planktivorous. Adults are primarily benthic and omnivorous, feeding on both plant and animal material.

Angling Importance: Although carp are generally considered a nuisance by North American anglers, they are highly prized as a sportfish in Europe, primarily because they are often excellent fighters. A growing number of anglers in the U.S. are becoming interested in carp as a sportfish, and although flavor often varies with the quality of the water from which fish were captured, their sheer abundance and ease of capture have made them an important food fish in some areas. The Texas rod-and-reel record is currently 25.6 pounds, and the bowfishing record is 41.75 pounds. The North American record exceeds 57 pounds.

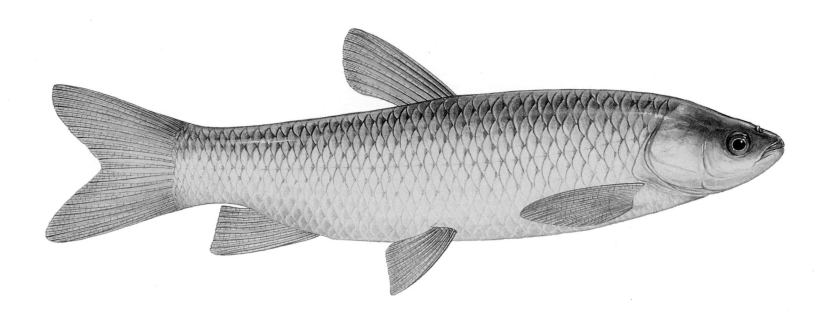

Grass Carp
Ctenopharyngodon idella (Valenciennes)

Other Names: White Amur, Waan ue

Grass Carp—*Ctenopharyngodon idella* (Valenciennes)

Distribution: Grass carp are native to large rivers in Asia, and range from the Amur River in China and Siberia, south to the West River in China and Thailand. Because of its utility as a food fish, the species has been cultured nearly worldwide. Also, because of its utility as a biological control for aquatic vegetation, the species has been legally introduced into at least 35 states in the U.S. Established, reproducing populations now occur in Mississippi River drainages. In Texas, triploid (sterile) grass carp have been widely introduced in small private ponds, and a few public waters, for vegetation control. Diploid (non-sterile) grass carp occur, and are reproducing in the Trinity River-Galveston Bay area. Diploid populations became established by escapees from either legal diploid experiments in Lake Conroe or from illegal stockings.

Description: *Ctenopharyngodon* and *idella* are both Greek words, meaning "comb-like throat-teeth" and "distinct," respectively. The grass carp is one of the largest members of the minnow family. The body is oblong with moderately large scales, while the head has no scales. There are three simple and seven branched rays on the dorsal fin. Grass carp are silvery to olive in color, lacking the golden hue of common carp. Grass carp have no barbels. This species typically reaches sizes

of 65–80 pounds in its native habitat, but individuals approaching 400 pounds have been reported.

Biology: Typically, spawning occurs in the spring when water temperatures reach 59–63°F, and under rising water conditions. Eggs are semi-pelagic and must remain suspended during the 20–40 hour incubation period. Therefore, long river stretches are usually necessary for successful spawning. Currently, only triploid (sterile) grass carp are legal for use in Texas, and a permit is required to obtain them. Once young grass carp reach approximately three inches in length, they become nearly 100% herbivorous. Their herbivorous feeding habits make them ideal as vegetation control agents since they are capable of consuming 40–300% of their body weight per day in plant material.

Angling Importance: Although grass carp may be landed occasionally by rod-and-reel anglers, their herbivorous feeding habits make them very difficult to catch. However, when they are landed they are excellent table fare despite their bones, and often command high prices at fish markets. The rod-and-reel record in Texas for grass carp stands at 42 pounds. However, a specimen in excess of 65 pounds was landed by a bowfisher.

Sterile grass carp are currently produced by subjecting newly fertilized eggs to pressure. Pressure shock causes the fertilized egg to retain a polar body, which means it will have three sets of chromosomes — a condition called **triploidy** — two from the female and one from the male, rather than one set from each parent. About 8,000 PSI for 1.5 minutes appears to be optimal for producing the highest percentages of triploidy and survival combined (Cassani and Caton 1986, personal communication).

Golden Shiner—*Notemigonus crysoleucas* (Mitchill)

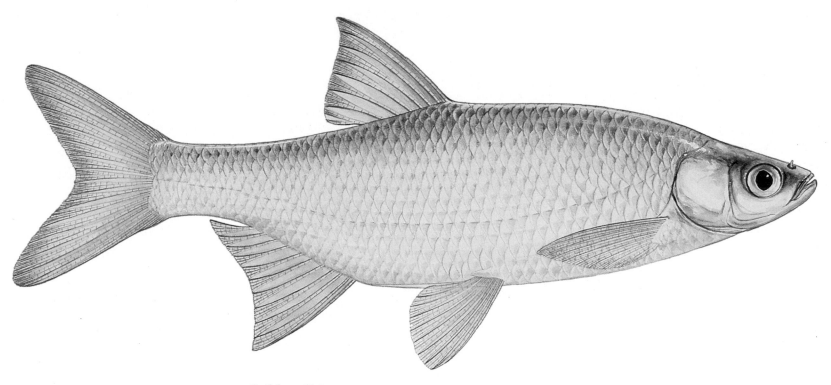

Golden Shiner
Notemigonus crysoleucas (Mitchill)

Other Names: None

Golden Shiner—*Notemigonus crysoleucas* [Mitchill]

Distribution: The golden shiner ranges over most of eastern North America. In the east the species is found from Nova Scotia south to Florida. In the central plains the species becomes very rare, especially west of a line extending from central Texas through central Montana. However, the species is well represented in parts of Arizona and California. In Texas the golden shiner is nearly ubiquitous, probably as a result of bait releases. It is believed to have been native only to east Texas streams.

Description: Both *Notemigonus* and *crysoleucas* are Greek, meaning "angled back" and "golden white" (a reference to the species color). The golden shiner is a deep-bodied minnow. There are 7–9 branched rays in the dorsal fin, and 8–19 branched rays in the anal fin. The mouth is small and upturned. The lateral line has a strong downward curve. The back is olive-green, with a darker stripe along the midline. The sides range in color from silver to gold.

Biology: Typically, golden shiners prefer water with little to no current. Spawning begins in the spring when water temperatures reach about 70°F, and ceases when temperatures exceed 80°F. Sometimes spawning resumes in late summer if water temperatures drop below 80°F. No nest is prepared. Adhesive eggs are scattered over algae or submerged vegetation and hatch in approximately 4 days (under good conditions). Golden shiners are omnivorous. About half the diet consists of plant material, and about half animal material such as crustaceans, insects and snails. In Texas, golden shiners in excess of 8 inches and weighing 0.25 pounds have been reported.

Angling Importance: Often used as a bait fish.

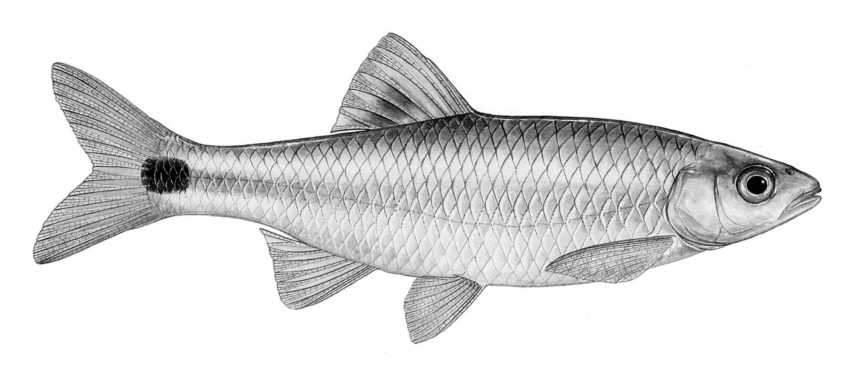

Blacktail Shiner
Cyprinella venusta (Girard)

Other Names: None

Blacktail Shiner—*Cyprinella venusta* (Girard)

Distribution: Blacktail shiners are found in the southern U.S. west of the Appalachian Mountains. The species ranges east and west from north-central Florida to west Texas, and north to southern Illinois. In Texas blacktail shiners are unknown in the Panhandle, being found primarily from the Edwards Plateau eastward.

Description: *Cyprinella* is Greek for "small carp" and *venusta* is Latin for "beautiful, like Venus." The blacktail shiner is a somewhat slender minnow with 8–9 rays on the anal fin, and a prominent black spot at the base of the tail fin. The back is usually yellowish-olive, and the sides are silvery with hints of blue.

Biology: Unlike the golden shiner, blacktail shiners prefer flowing waters. They are usually most abundant in areas with little vegetation, swift current, and gravelly bottoms. Adults in Texas have reached 4.6 inches in length.

Angling Importance: None.

 Did You Know?
When streams are modified by engineers to reduce bank erosion, stream width is extremely important. Making the stream wider isn't necessarily better. If banks are too far apart, unwanted deposition may occur. Water then moves faster because it must travel in smaller channels between sediment deposits, and bank erosion may actually increase.

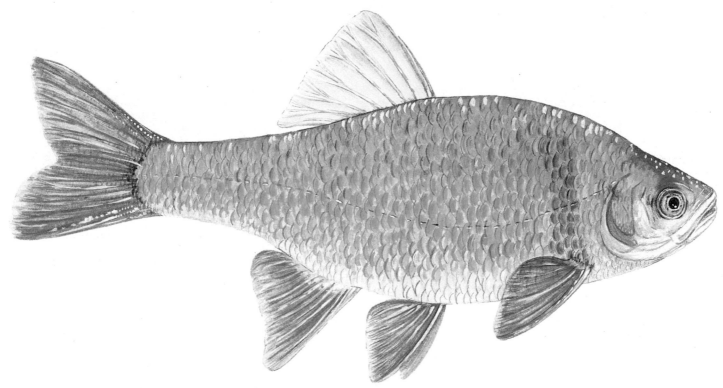

Red Shiner
Cyprinella lutrensis (Baird and Girard)

Other Names: Red-horse minnow

Red Shiner—*Cyprinella lutrensis* (Baird and Girard)

Distribution: The red shiner is native to central North America west of the Mississippi River drainage, ranging as far west as New Mexico. Latitudinally the species ranges from central Mexico north to South Dakota. Clearly a plains species, red shiners range throughout Texas. One subspecies, *Cyprinella lutrensis blairi*, formerly found in the Big Bend region, is thought to be extinct.

Description: *Cyprinella* is Greek for "small carp" and *lutrensis* is derived from the Latin lutra which means "otter," a reference to Otter Creek, Arkansas, where the species was first captured. Coloration is similar to the blacktail shiner, olive-green above and silvery on the sides. Spawning males become blueish on the sides and the fins redden. There are 7-8 rays in the dorsal fin. The anal fin has 8-10 rays (usually 9). Maximum size is only about 3.5 inches. The species is sometimes confused with golden shiners, and exotic minnows such as the rudd *Scardinius erythrophthalmus* (native to Europe through Asia Minor) or the roach *Rutilus rutilus* (native to Europe and Asia).

Biology: The red shiner spawns over an extended period of time from spring into fall months, with a peak from early to mid-summer. Spawning may occur on riffles, on or near submerged objects, over vegetation beds or in association with sunfish nests. Adults typically school in midwater or near the surface. The species is thought to feed primarily on small invertebrates.

Angling Importance: Often used as a bait fish.

Aquatic plants offer habitat for a wide variety of fish food organisms. For example, up to 60% of the invertebrates in some aquatic systems are found in association with plants. Additionally, for many small fish, plants offer a refuge from predation by larger fish.

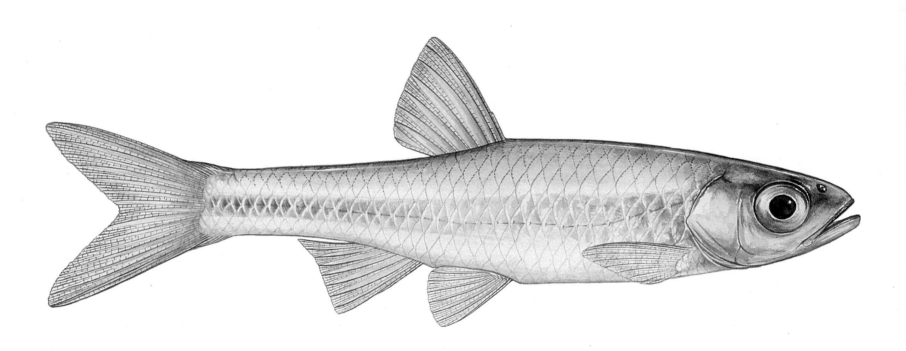

Texas Shiner
Notropis amabilis (Girard)

Other Names: None

Texas Shiner—*Notropis amabilis* [Girard]

Distribution: The species range includes portions of Mexico as well as Texas. In Texas it is found primarily in Edwards Plateau streams from the San Gabriel River in the east to the Pecos River in the west. In Mexico the species is found in Rio Grande tributaries including Rio Salado and Rio San Juan.

Description: *Notropis* is Greek for "back keel" and *amabilis* is Latin for "lovely." The Texas shiner is distinguished by large eyes, black lips and a clear stripe just above a black stripe along its side. The stripe is most distinct toward the rear of the fish, close to the tail fin. There are 9 rays on the anal fin.

Biology: Typical habitat includes rocky or sandy runs, as well as pools. Texas shiners are predaceous and it is believed the large eyes are an adaptation for sight feeding in swift water. The species is typically found in schools, with individuals as large as 2.5 inches. Spawning behavior has not been studied.

Angling Importance: None.

The term **plankton** refers to plants and animals (usually very small, or microscopic) that float or drift in the water. Also included are very weak swimming organisms that are carried along in the current. Planktonic plants are called phytoplankton and animals are called zooplankton. Most newly hatched fish rely on plankton as a food source. Some filter-feeders such as shad continue to utilize plankton as adults.

Fathead Minnow—*Pimephales promelas* (Rafinesque)

Fathead Minnow
Pimephales promelas (Rafinesque)

Other Names: Fathead

Fathead Minnow—*Pimephales promelas* (Rafinesque)

Distribution: The fathead minnow may be found throughout much of North America east of the Rocky Mountains from Mexico into the Great Slave Lake drainage of northern Canada, with the notable exception of southern portions of the Atlantic coastal plain. The species is found nearly statewide in Texas, presumably as a result of bait releases.

Description: *Pimephales* and *promelas* are both Greek words, meaning "fathead" and "before black," respectively. The fathead minnow has a rounded snout and short rounded fins. There is a dark spot at the base of the tail fin, and sometimes there is a blotch on the anterior portion of the dorsal fin. As with many other minnows there is a darkening along the midline of the back. The anal fin has 7 rays.

Biology: The fathead minnow is a stream fish, able to tolerate a wide range of environmental conditions including high temperature, low oxygen levels, and high turbidities. The species seems to be most abundant in small streams where competition with other species is limited. Fathead minnows school either in midwater or near the bottom, and feed primarily on plant material, although invertebrates are sometimes consumed. Spawning is prolonged from late spring through mid-summer. Eggs are deposited over submerged objects and guarded by males. Nests may contain as many as 12,000 eggs, and females may spawn as many as 12 times during a single summer. Some individuals may mature and spawn during their first summer of life. However, spawning is usually delayed until the second summer. Because of its prolific nature in the absence of competition, fathead minnows are often raised in ponds for sale as a baitfish, or as forage in hatchery production ponds.

Angling Importance: Often used as a bait fish.

Did You Know?
Koi carp, fathead minnows, and goldfish among others may be used as forage fishes in hatchery rearing ponds.

Gizzard Shad—*Dorosoma cepedianum* (Lesueur)

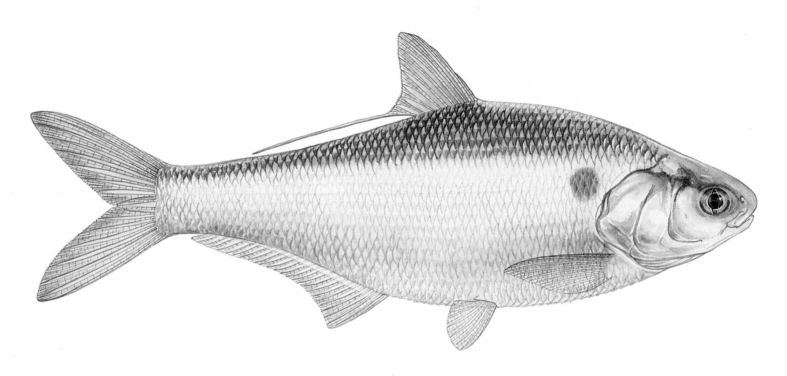

Gizzard Shad
Dorosoma cepedianum (Lesueur)

Other Names: Shad, hickory shad, herring, skipjack

Gizzard Shad—*Dorosoma cepedianum* [Lesueur]

Distribution: Gizzard shad are native to eastern North America. In the north the range includes the Saint Lawrence River, the Great Lakes (exclusive of Lake Superior), and extends west into North Dakota. Gizzard shad are found as far south as eastern Mexico, and as far west as New Mexico. The species is not found in New England, south Florida, or through most of the Appalachian Mountain chain. In Texas gizzard shad are found in all major streams and reservoirs.

Description: *Dorosoma* is Greek for "lance body," referring to the lance-like shape of young shad. The species epithet *cepedianum* refers to the French naturalist Citoyen Lacépède. Gizzard shad are usually easily distinguished from threadfin shad by the fact that the upper jaw projects well beyond the lower jaw. Amateur ichthyologists can run a finger underneath the mouth forward, and if the fingernail catches on the upper jaw and opens the mouth, in most cases the fish is a gizzard rather than a threadfin shad. Additionally, the anal fin usually has 29–35 rays, as opposed to 20–25 rays found in threadfin shad. The upper surface is silvery-blue, and grades to nearly white on the sides and belly. Fins do not have the yellowing tint present in threadfin shad. Unlike threadfin shad, the chin and floor of the mouth is not speckled with black pigment.

Biology: Gizzard shad are most abundant in large rivers and reservoirs, avoiding high gradient streams. The species is most often found in large schools. The common name "skipjack" is derived from the fact that individuals within a school may often be observed leaping out of the water, or skipping along the surface on their sides. Spawning generally takes place in late spring, usually in shallow protected water. Eggs and milt are released in the school, seemingly without regard for individual mates. Adhesive eggs attach to submerged objects and hatch in about 4 days. Although adult shad are moderately deep-bodied, fry are extremely slender and delicate looking until they reach about 1.25 inches in length. Gizzard shad are planktivorous. Young feed on microscopic animals and plants, as well as small insect larvae. Adults feed by filtering small food items from the water using their long close-set gill rakers. Although the species commonly grows to lengths of 9–14 inches, some have been reported to exceed 20 inches in length. In Texas the record (taken with a speargun) is an 18.25 inch specimen that weighed in at nearly three (2.97) pounds.

Angling Importance: Gizzard shad provide forage for most game species. They rarely bite on a hook, and when they do (or are snagged) they are generally considered to be worthless as a food fish. The soft flesh is not only tasteless, but quick to rot. However, the species is often used as cut bait for other fish species.

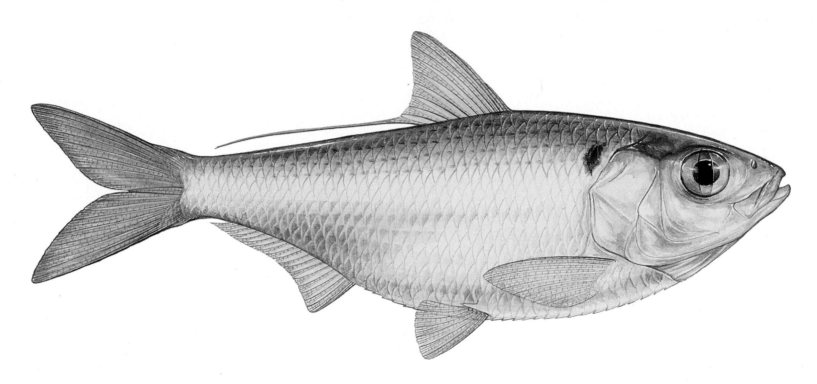

Threadfin Shad
Dorosoma petenense (Gunther)

Other Names: None

Threadfin Shad—*Dorosoma petenense* [Gunther]

Distribution: Threadfin shad naturally occur in waters west of the Appalachian Mountains, north to Kentucky, west to east Texas, south to the Rio Grande drainage, and east to Florida. The species has been widely introduced in California and Arizona, as well as Appalachian and southern Atlantic states. Threadfin shad are common in all east Texas streams, and have been introduced as a forage fish in many reservoirs statewide.

Description: *Dorosoma* is Greek for "lance body," referring to the lance-like shape of young shad. The word *petenense* refers to Lake Peten in the Yucatan, the species type locality. Threadfin shad are usually easily distinguished from gizzard shad by the fact that the upper jaw does not project beyond the lower jaw. Additionally, the anal fin usually has 20–25 rays, as opposed to 29–35 rays found in gizzard shad. The upper surface is silvery-blue, and grades to nearly white on the sides and belly. All fins have yellow tint except the dorsal. Unlike gizzard shad, the chin and floor of the mouth is speckled with black pigment in threadfin shad.

Biology: Like gizzard shad, threadfin shad are most commonly found in large rivers and reservoirs. However, threadfin shad are more likely to be found in waters with a noticeable current and are usually found in the upper five feet of water. Additionally, threadfin shad are quite temperature sensitive with die-offs reported at temperatures below 45°F. Spawning begins in the spring when water temperatures reach approximately 70°F, and may continue into the summer. During spawning one or more females are accompanied by several males. Adults are considerably smaller than gizzard shad adults and rarely exceed 6 inches in length.

Angling Importance: Often used as a bait fish. Threadfin shad almost never bite on a hook and no angling records are available.

Texas is divided into 15 management districts. TPWD personnel in each district collect valuable information about fish population size and composition in many targeted lakes. Most lakes are **surveyed** for this information every three years, whereas others are surveyed on an annual basis.

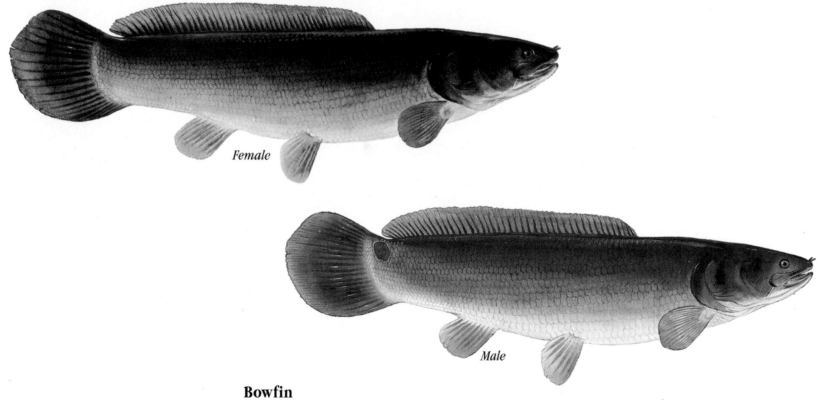

Female

Male

Bowfin
Amia calva (Linnaeus)

Other Names: Grindle, dogfish, grinnel, cypress trout, mud fish

Bowfin—*Amia calva* (Linnaeus)

Distribution: With the exception of the Appalachian Mountains, the bowfin is native to the eastern U.S., ranging from extreme southeastern Canada to the Gulf Coast. In Texas the species is found in the Red River, San Jacinto River and Sabine River systems, as well as the downstream reaches of the Brazos and Colorado rivers.

Description: *Amia* is a Greek name for an unidentified fish, probably the bonito, and *calva* is Latin meaning "smooth," referring perhaps to the fish's scaleless head. The bowfin has a large mouth equipped with many sharp teeth. Its large head has no scales. The dorsal fin is long, extending more than half the length of the back, and contains more than 45 rays. None of the fins have spines. The tail is rounded, and the backbone extends part way into it. There is a barbel-like flap associated with each nostril. The back is mottled olive-green shading to lighter green on the belly. There is a difference in color among the fins. The dorsal is dark green, while all others are light green (coinciding perhaps with overall body color changes). Young fish have a distinctive black spot near the base of the upper portions of the tail fin. The spot is usually margined with yellow or orange. Although it persists in adult fish it is less prominent in females.

Biology: Bowfins spawn in the late spring. Nests are constructed by males in shallow, weedy areas. Vegetation and silt are removed from the nest by males and the adhesive eggs attach to any hard structure that is left, such as roots, gravel, wood, etc. Eggs hatch in 8–10 days. Males guard both incubating eggs and fry which may remain in the nest for about nine days after hatching. Initially, bowfin young feed on small invertebrates such as cladocerans (water fleas). However, by the time they reach about four inches in length they are primarily piscivorous, although crayfish can make up a substantial proportion of the diet, and frogs are also consumed. Young fish may grow as much as 12–14 inches during their first year. Bowfins tend to be found in deeper water during the day, and migrate into shallower areas to feed at night. Their swim bladder is used as a lung and they may be seen surfacing to renew their air supply from time to time. In general, the average size in Texas is six to eight pounds.

Angling Importance: Although bowfins are not usually sought after in Texas, it is generally acknowledged that once hooked they are excellent fighters. Indeed, some anglers relish the thought of hooking a bowfin. Relative to consumption, bowfins are typically considered a rough fish rather than one for the table.

However, some anglers eat them with enthusiasm. The flesh is somewhat softer than that of sunfish, but the flavor has been compared to shark meat. The state record is 17.65 pounds.

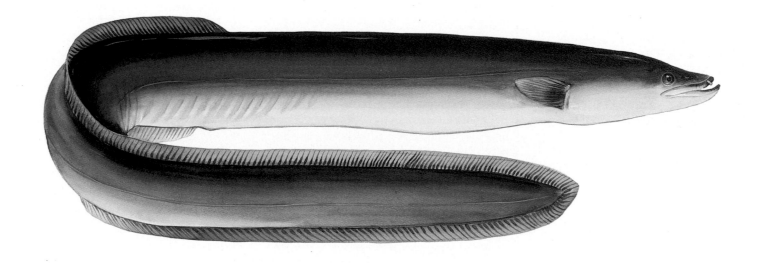

American Eel
Anguilla rostrata (Lesueur)

Other Names: Freshwater eel

American Eel—*Anguilla rostrata* (Lesueur)

Distribution: The American eel occurs in a variety of habitats, and is probably the most wide-ranging fish latitudinally in North America. This species is known from Greenland to as far south as Brazil. American eels occur as far west as New Mexico, and are common throughout the Caribbean and the West Indies. Although native to much of Texas, the construction of dams, which impede upstream spawning migrations, has eliminated this species from most central and western areas of the state.

Description: *Anguilla* and *rostrata* are both Latin, meaning "eel" and "beaked," respectively. The latter is probably a reference to the fish's snout. The American eel has a slender snake-like body with very small scales, and the fish may appear naked. A long dorsal fin usually extends for more than half the length of the body and is continuous with a similar ventral fin. Pelvic fins are absent. The back may be olive-green to brown shading to greenish-yellow on the sides and light gray or white on the belly.

Biology: The American eel, as well as the European eel, spawns during the winter in the Sargasso Sea, a tropical area northeast of Cuba. Adult eels spend most of their lives in freshwater, although the amount of time may vary among individuals. At some point, however, adults leave their freshwater habitats and move toward the Sargasso Sea. Neither adults or eggs have been collected in the vicinity of the Sargasso Sea, but newly hatched eels are found there. Presumably, spawning takes place in deep water and the adults die shortly thereafter. Young eels are transparent and leaf shaped. Years ago when they were first collected they were thought to be a new fish species and erroneously given the scientific name *Leptocephalus*. Within about a year, growing and moving toward the mainland, the American eels transform into more eel-like forms called "glass eels" or "elvers" and are ready to enter freshwater (European eels have a much longer journey and the process takes about three years). By the time American eels get close to the coast they are about 6 inches in length. The species only begins to develop coloration when the young reach nearshore areas. Once they reach freshwater, females continue to migrate deep inland as far up rivers and tributaries as they can. Males remain much closer to coastline areas. Eels tend to hide under rocks or submerged rocks, during the day, and venture out only at night to feed.

Angling Importance: Although many anglers are put off by the snake-like appearance of eels, and the prodigious amounts of slime they produce when captured, eels are in fact an exceptionally good food fish. In Texas eels are usually caught by anglers fishing for something else. The unrestricted state record is 4.22 pounds and over three feet in length (38 inches). The world record is 8.5 pounds.

Chain Pickerel
Esox niger (Lesueur)

Other Names: Pike, jackfish

Chain Pickerel—*Esox niger* (Lesueur)

Distribution: Chain pickerel are distributed along the Atlantic Coast of North America from New Brunswick and Nova Scotia south to Florida. The species is found in the Mississippi River drainage from the Gulf Coast as far north as Illinois and Indiana, and may be found in Gulf drainages as far west as the Sabine and Red rivers in Texas.

Description: *Esox* and *niger* are both Latin words. *Esox* means "pike," and *niger* means "dark," or "black." Like its close relatives, northern pike and muskellunge, the chain pickerel is equipped with a large mouth, well adapted for piscivory. The lower jaw, which extends further forward than the upper jaw, is equipped with four sensory pores on the underside. The dorsal and anal fins are set well back on the body. Chain pickerel are usually olive-green or yellowish-brown on the back and sides, shading to a creamy yellow underneath. There is a distinctive pattern of interlocking dark bands on the back and sides that is reminiscent of a chain-link fence.

Biology: In Texas chain pickerel spawn between December and February. Strings of sticky eggs are deposited on aquatic vegetation and subsequently fertilized. There is no parental care. When the young hatch they feed on plankton, aquatic insects or even their own siblings. At about three inches the diet becomes almost exclusively other fish. Individuals that shift to a diet of fish earliest tend to grow faster. The species prefers cover and is most often found in patches of aquatic vegetation. In general, they lie in wait and strike when unsuspecting prey swim their way. During their first year they may reach 12-14 inches in length. Growth slows somewhat during the second year when they may attain lengths of 1.5 feet. In Texas they typically reach sizes of 3-4 pounds and about 2 feet in length.

Angling Importance: Fishing for chain pickerel is basically a winter-time activity in Texas. It begins with the first real cold front in the fall and continues until March or April when water temperatures warm. Like northern pike, chain pickerel are bony, but usually considered tasty. Although the national record is over nine pounds, the Texas state record is 4.63 pounds (25 inches).

Fish are often sampled in shallow water using electricity. **Electric current** is used to either stun fish, or to force them to swim toward an electrode. After they are collected, weighed and measured, most fish are returned to the water essentially unharmed.

Rainbow Trout
Oncorhynchus mykiss (Walbaum)

Other Names: None

Rainbow Trout—*Oncorhynchus mykiss* (Walbaum)

Distribution: Rainbow trout are native to North America west of the Rockies from Alaska into northwestern Mexico. Introductions have extended the range to include the Great Lakes region, south-central Canada and portions of the Great Plains east of the Rocky Mountains, and southwestern Mexico. Although the species has been widely introduced in Texas to provide winter-time "put-and-take" fisheries, the only self-sustaining population in the state exists in McKittrick Canyon in the Guadalupe Mountains.

Description: *Oncorhynchus* is Greek meaning "hook snout," and *mykiss* is the Kamchatkan name for rainbow trout. Rainbow trout have a characteristic salmonid (salmon-like) shape. Dark spots are clearly visible on the tail fin which is slightly forked. The anal fin has 10–12 rays. The back is usually a dark olive color, shading to silvery white on the underside. The body is heavily speckled, and there is a pink to red stripe running lengthwise along the fish's sides.

Biology: Rainbow trout are a cool-to-cold-water fish species. Although they have been known to tolerate higher temperatures, they do best in areas where the temperature remains below 70°F. In Texas high temperatures prevent reproduction or even over-summer survival in most areas (some may survive the summer in tailrace areas below large dams such as at Canyon Reservoir). Successful spawning has been reported only from the Guadalupe Mountains. Eggs are laid in shallow nests dug out by the female in gravel riffles. The eggs require continuous oxygenation. At temperatures of about 55°F, the eggs will hatch approximately 21 days after they are laid. Rainbow trout are carnivores, but not exclusively piscivorous. They feed on a wide variety of prey including insects, crustaceans, mollusks and fish. Rainbows with access to the sea (the species is anadromous) have been known to exceed 42 pounds. The record size for those confined to freshwater is 31.37 pounds.

Angling Importance: Since rainbow trout generally do not reproduce in Texas, and are unable to survive through the summer in most areas, the species is primarily used in winter put-and-take fisheries. Each winter several hundred thousand rainbows are stocked in community fishing lakes around the state. Generally, they are stocked at 8–9 inches in length. Much enthusiasm is generated by the annual stockings. On occasion banks are lined with anglers eager to catch their limit of trout immediately after they are stocked. The state record is 7.77 pounds and was taken from Canyon Reservoir tailrace.

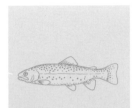

Cold-water fish such as **trout** may survive the summer in tailrace areas below large dams, because water entering the tailrace is drawn from deeper cooler water near the dam. Such water may remain cool even during hot months of the year. However, in some situations, low oxygen levels can become a problem in these areas.

Paddlefish
Polyodon spathula (Walbaum)

Other Names: Spoonbill, spoonbill cat, shovelnose cat, boneless cat

Paddlefish—*Polyodon spathula* [Walbaum]

Distribution: Paddlefish are native to Lake Erie, the Mississippi River drainage including the upper stretches of the Missouri and Ohio rivers, and adjacent Gulf slope drainages from the San Jacinto River in Texas to the Mobile Bay area in Alabama. Once common throughout their range, overfishing and habitat degradation have led to drastic declines in recent years (e.g., although once reported from Ontario the species has been extirpated from Canada). In Texas paddlefish were once found in every major river from the Trinity River eastward. However, by the 1950s their numbers and range had been substantially reduced. Within the state they are considered an endangered species, and a paddlefish restoration program has been initiated by the Texas Parks and Wildlife Department.

Description: *Polyodon* is a Greek word meaning "many tooth," and refers to the species' many gill rakers; *spathula* is Latin for "spatula" or "blade," and is an obvious reference to the fish's snout. The paddlefish may be distinguished from all other species by the broad, flat, bill-like snout (paddle). The paddle may be half as long as the body. Minus the long snout, the paddlefish superficially resembles a shark. The tail is deeply forked, and the color is gray. However, paddlefish skin is smooth and scaleless. Underneath the snout

the mouth is large and dangerous looking, but has no teeth.

Biology: In Texas, paddlefish spawn from early spring through early summer. Fish move upstream into spawning areas when the water temperature reaches about 50°F. Fast flowing water (floods which last several days), and clean sand or gravel bottoms are required for successful spawning. During spawning paddlefish gather in schools. Details are not well understood, but it is believed several males accompany a female. Eggs and sperm are released as the fish swim over suitable habitat. The eggs are sticky and adhere to solid objects (such as rocks). Incubation takes about nine days at 57°F. The snout does not become prominent for several weeks after the fry hatch. Young fish grow quickly. Growth of six inches or more has been reported in several months, 12 to 14 inches is typical for the first year, but growth potential is even higher. Fish less than one and a half years old have attained lengths of three feet in controlled pond situations. Generally, fish become sexually mature at 5-10 years of age, and may live to be 20-30 years old. Although the large mouth is imposing, paddlefish are harmless plankton feeders inhabiting open water, for the most part, where they can filter large quantities of water for plankton. Fish commonly reach sizes

of 40-60 pounds, but specimens over seven feet long and weighing over 160 pounds have been reported.

Angling Importance: At one time the paddlefish fishery was a booming business, however, population declines forced a moratorium on harvest in most areas. In Texas no paddlefish may be caught, for either commercial or recreational purposes, until population abundance, and reproductive success have improved enough to re-open the fishery.

The snout, or paddle, is long and flat (opposite, top), with the underside (opposite, bottom) dotted with sensory pits to locate plankton as the fish feeds with its enormous mouth agape (below)

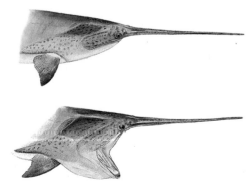

Greenthroat Darter—*Etheostoma lepidum* (Baird and Girard)

Greenthroat Darter
Etheostoma lepidum (Baird and Girard)

Other Names: None

Greenthroat Darter—*Etheostoma lepidum* (Baird and Girard)

Distribution: The greenthroat darter is known only from the Pecos River system in southeastern New Mexico, and from the Edwards Plateau region in central Texas.

Description: *Etheostoma* is derived from two Greek words, *etheo* meaning "to strain" and *stoma* meaning "mouth;" *lepidum* is Greek for "pretty." Greenthroat darters are among the most colorful of North American fishes. They grow to be about 2.5 inches in length. Males have red to orange spots between green bars on their sides. Females have yellow between short brown to black bars. Males also have green pelvic and anal fins, with green in the throat area.

Biology: Greenthroat darters are winter spawners. Spawning seems to begin sometime in October and end in May. During that time females may produce 30–39 groups of eggs. Greenthroat darters typically inhabit riffles with gravel substrate. Spring-fed streams and vegetated riffles appear to be preferred. Food preferences and growth rate are less well understood.

Angling Importance: None.

Bluegreen algae (cyanobacteria) can grow to high levels in nutrient-rich waters, becoming a nuisance for boaters, anglers and other users. Although bluegreens are **photosynthetic** like algae, they are actually very closely related to bacteria. Like bacteria, and unlike true algae and higher plants and animals, bluegreens' genetic material is not contained within a cell nucleus.

Walleye
Stizostedion vitreum (Mitchill)

Other Names: Walleyed pike, pike

Walleye—*Stizostedion vitreum* (Mitchill)

Distribution: The walleye is native to the central portion of North America from the Rocky Mountain to the Appalachian Mountain chains, ranging as far south as Arkansas, Mississippi and Alabama, and as far north as Great Slave Lake, the Mackenzie River and the Peace River in northwest Canada. Introductions have extended the range beyond the Appalachian Mountains in the east, to the Columbia River in the west, and as far south as Texas. Walleyes have been stocked in numerous Texas reservoirs.

Description: *Stizostedion* is Greek, and *vitreum* is Latin, meaning "pungent throat" and "glass," respectively. The latter is probably a reference to the species large eyes. As is typical of perches, the walleye is equipped with two separate dorsal fins. The anterior fin has spines, and the posterior dorsal fin has soft rays (19-22). The anal fin has 12–14 rays and two spines. The body is generally mottled with dark blotches on a yellowish-to-greenish brown background. Colors on the lower body shade to white on the belly. The lower lobe of the tail fin has a light tip. Walleyes are obvious carnivores with teeth in the jaws and on the roof of the mouth.

Biology: Walleyes are early spring spawners. They are generally nocturnal with most activity, including spawning, occurring at night. In the spring, spawning begins when water temperatures reach 45–50°F. Fish begin to move upstream into tributaries. Typically, spawning takes place on riffles after fish have moved upstream, but in lakes spawning may also take place on rip-rap dams or reefs (as in the Great Lakes). Eggs are scattered at random by females who are accompanied by several males that fertilize the eggs. Walleye eggs are adhesive and stick to the substrate. At water temperatures of 57°F they hatch in about seven days. There is no nest building, and no parental care for eggs or fry. Young walleyes are fast growers and may attain lengths of 10 inches or more during their first year if conditions are favorable. Although young fish may consume crustaceans and various insects and their larvae, adults are primarily piscivorous. Walleyes typically live to be 7–8 years old and weigh 12–15 pounds. However, individuals in their mid "teens" have been collected, and the world all-tackle record is 25 pounds.

Angling Importance: High summer water temperatures restrict walleye growth and survival in much of Texas. However, in north Texas lakes such as Lake Meredith the species does very well. Six-to-eight-pound specimens are common at times. The state record comes from Lake Meredith and stands at 11.88 pounds. Walleyes are considered an excellent food fish from Texas to the northern states.

Inland Silverside
Menidia beryllina (Cope)

Other Names: None

Inland Silverside—*Menidia beryllina* (Cope)

Distribution: The inland silverside is native to Atlantic and Gulf Coast estuaries and associated upstream freshwaters from Massachusetts to the Rio Grande. The species has been found in the Mississippi River drainage as far north as Illinois. The species has also been collected from the Pecos River in New Mexico. Inland silversides are found in many Texas reservoirs.

Description: *Menidia* is Greek, meaning "moon." In ancient times meni was the name given to small silvery fish. The Greek word *beryllina* means "a sea-green jewel." Formerly known as the "tidewater silverside," the inland silverside is synonymous with *Menidia audens*. The species is quite slender, with a silvery color, and a somewhat pointed snout. The front of the first dorsal fin is well ahead of the front of the anal fin. The anal fin usually has 15–20 rays, less than the brook silverside, *Labidesthes sicculus*, which typically has 22–25 anal fin rays. There is a bright silvery stripe running horizontally along the sides. The belly is nearly white.

Biology: In Texas, the inland silverside may spawn from early spring through mid-summer. Although the life history is not well documented, research from Lake Texoma, Texas, indicates that eggs are laid in algae associated with emergent vegetation. The normal life span

appears to be less than 1.5 years; however, two-year-old females are occasionally collected. Maximum size is about three inches.

Angling Importance: None.

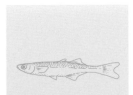

Following the removal of vegetation in Lake Conroe, Texas, by the introduction of 270,000 grass carp in the early 1980s, there was a corresponding increase in the ratio of **inland silversides** to **brook silversides** (Bettoli et al 1991).

Western Mosquitofish—*Gambusia affinis* (Baird and Girard)

Western Mosquitofish
Gambusia affinis (Baird and Girard)

Other Names: Gambusia

Western Mosquitofish—*Gambusia affinis* (Baird and Girard)

Distribution: The western mosquitofish naturally ranges in central North America, east of the Rockies and west of the Appalachian Mountains, as far north as Illinois and south to Veracruz, Mexico. Introductions have occurred as far north as southern Canada and as far west as California. Worldwide, the species has been widely introduced for mosquito control. In Texas various species of mosquitofish are common in many locations and occur throughout the state.

Description: *Gambusia* is derived from the Cuban word "gambusino." The Latin word *affinis* means "related." Gambusia are small fish less than three inches in length. The mouth is strongly upturned and the tail fin is rounded. The back and sides are yellowish-brown, and there is a dusky V-shaped bar beneath the eye.

Biology: Gambusia spawn during warm months of the year. Each female may produce three or four broods. Throughout the spawning season males pursue females. Fertilization is internal. Gambusia are livebearers, with a gestation period of 21–28 days. The number of young in a single brood may range from a few to over three hundred. The species' food habits are quite diverse, including animals (insects, crustaceans, mollusks, rotifers, etc.)

as well as algae, with mosquito larvae being the preferred food item.

Angling Importance: May be used as a bait fish.

anadromous	migrating from salt water into freshwater, for breeding purposes
anterior	the head end of an animal, or toward that portion of the body (front)
benthic	living at or near the bottom
cladoceran	one of several major types of planktonic crustaceans, sometimes called "water fleas"
detritus	loose material that results from wearing away or decomposition
distal	situated away from the point of origin or attachment of a fin or other appendage
dorsal	toward, or having to do with the back or upper surface of an animal
invertebrate	an animal lacking a spinal column
omnivorous	feeding on both animal and vegetable matter
opercle	bony covering of a fish's gills
oxbow lake	a lake formed when a portion of a meandering river or stream becomes separated and cut off from the main channel
piscivory or piscivorous	feeding on fishes
posterior	the rear or tail portion of an animal, or toward the rear portion of the body (rear)
rotifer	a microscopic animal that bears circles of tiny beating "hairs" (cilia) that give the appearance of rotating wheels
semi-pelagic	only partially equipped for survival in open ocean waters
turbid	unclear, murky, or opaque
ubiquitous	being everywhere, or found everywhere
ventral	toward, or having to do with the belly or lower surface of an animal

Bettoli, P.W., J.E Morris and R.L. Noble. 1991. Changes in the abundance of two atherinid species after aquatic vegetation removal. *Transactions of the American Fisheries Society 120:90-97.*

Cassani, J.R. and W.E. Caton. 1986. Efficient production of triploid grass carp (*Ctenopharyngodon idella*) utilizing hydrostatic pressure. *Aquaculture 55:43-50.*

Clay, W.M. 1962. *A field manual of Kentucky fishes.* Kentucky Department of Fish and Wildlife Resources, Frankfort, Kentucky.

Coble, D.W. 1975. Smallmouth bass. **In** Stroud, R.H. and H. Clepper (eds.) *Black Bass Biology and Management.* Sport Fishing Institute, Washington, D.C.

Heidinger, R.C. 1975. Life history and biology of the largemouth bass. **In** Stroud, R.H. and H. Clepper (eds.) *Black Bass Biology and Management.* Sport Fishing Institute, Washington, D.C.

Howells, R.G. 1992. *Guide to identification of harmful and potentially harmful fishes, shellfishes and aquatic plants prohibited in Texas.* Texas Parks and Wildlife Department, Special Publication PWD-BK-N3200-376, Austin, Texas.

Hubbs, C., R.J. Edwards and G.P. Garrett. 1991. An annotated checklist of the freshwater fishes of Texas, with keys to identification of species. *Texas Journal of Science, Supplement, Volume 43:1-56.*

Hubbs, C., M.M. Stevenson and A.E. Peden. 1968. Fecundity and egg size in two central Texas darter populations. *The Southwestern Naturalist 13(3):301-324.*

Hurst, H., G. Bass and C. Hubbs. 1975. The biology of the Guadalupe, Suwannee and redeye basses. **In** Stroud, R.H. and H. Clepper (eds.) *Black Bass Biology and Management.* Sport Fishing Institute, Washington, D.C.

International Game Fish Association. 1991. *World record game fishes.* The International Game Fish Association, Fort Lauderdale, Florida.

Kemp, R.J., Jr. 1971. *Freshwater Fishes of Texas.* Texas Parks and Wildlife Department, Austin, Texas.

Lee, D.S., C.R. Gilbert, C.H. Hocutt, R.E. Jenkins, D.E. McAllister and J.R. Stauffer. 1980. *Atlas of North American Freshwater Fishes.* North Carolina Biological Survey.

McLarney, W. 1984. *The Freshwater Aquaculture Book: a Handbook for small scale Fish Culture in North America.* Hartley and Marks, Inc., Point Roberts, Washington.

National Fresh Water Fishing Hall of Fame. 1995. *Official world and USA state fresh water angling records.* National Fresh Water Fishing Hall of Fame, Hayward, Wisconsin.

Noakes, D.L.G. and E.K. Balon. 1982. Life Histories of Tilapias: An evolutionary perspective. **In** Pullin, R.S.V. and R.H. Lowe-McConnell (eds.) *The Biology and Culture of Tilapias.* International Center for Living Aquatic Resources Management, Manila, Philippines.

Oates, D.W., L.M. Krings and K. L. Ditz. 1993. *Field manual for the identification of selected North American freshwater fish by fillets and scales.* Nebraska Technical Series No. 19. Nebraska Game and Parks Commission, Lincoln, Nebraska.

Page, L.M. and B.M. Burr. 1991. *A Field Guide to Freshwater Fishes.* Houghton Mifflin Company, Boston, Massachusetts.

Pflieger, W.L. 1975. *The Fishes of Missouri.* Missouri Department of Conservation.

Philippart, J-Cl and J-Cl Ruwet. 1982. Ecology and distribution of tilapias. **In** Pullin, R.S.V. and R.H. Lowe-McConnell (eds.) *The Biology and Culture of Tilapias.* International Center for Living Aquatic Resources Management, Manila, Philippines.

Robins, R.C., R.M. Bailey, C.E. Bond, J.R. Brooker, E.A. Lachner, R.N. Lea and W.B. Scott. 1991. *Common and Scientific Names of Fishes from the United States and Canada.* American Fisheries Society Special Publication 20. Bethesda, Maryland.

Trewavas, E. 1982. Tilapias: Taxonomy and Speciation. **In** Pullin, R.S.V. and R.H. Lowe-McConnell (eds.) *The Biology and Culture of Tilapias.* International Center for Living Aquatic Resources Management, Manila, Philippines.

Vogele, L.E. 1975. The Spotted Bass. **In** Stroud, R.H. and H. Clepper (eds.) *Black Bass Biology and Management.* Sport Fishing Institute, Washington, D.C.

Useful comments and information provided by Dr. Gary Garrett of TPWD's Heart of the Hills field station, Ingram, Texas, were greatly appreciated. Additionally, I would like to thank Dr. Clark Hubbs of the University of Texas at Austin for verifying the accuracy of the illustrations.